The Shadow of the Cross

-Book Four-

E. G. White

AMAZING FACTS
MINISTRIES
For more info:
Call 1-888-402-6070
www.amazingfactsministries.com

PO Box 449
Creston, BC
V0B 1G0

Remnant
Publications

Coldwater, MI 49036

www.remnantpublications.com

Shadow of the Cross

Now is the TIME to Know

The Bible is as relevant as ever to your life and family.
Let us prove it! Our Bible Study Guides will help you
understand the Bible better than you ever have before ...

Find the answers you need!

Contents

1

The Good Samaritan

This chapter is based on Luke 10:25-37.

In the story of the good Samaritan, Christ illustrates the nature of true religion. He shows that it consists not in systems, creeds, or rites, but in the performance of loving deeds, in bringing the greatest good to others, in genuine goodness.

As Christ was teaching the people, "a certain lawyer stood up, and tempted Him, saying, Master, what shall I do to inherit eternal life?" With breathless attention the large congregation awaited the answer. The priests and rabbis had thought to entangle Christ by having the lawyer ask this question. But the Saviour entered into no controversy. He required the answer from the questioner himself. "What is written in the law?" He said; "how readest thou?" The Jews still accused Jesus of lightly regarding the law given from Sinai; but He turned the question of salvation upon the keeping of God's commandments.

The lawyer said, "Thou shalt love the Lord thy God with all thy heart, and with all thy soul, and with all thy strength, and with all thy mind; and thy neighbor as thyself." Jesus said, "Thou hast answered right: this do, and thou shalt live."

The lawyer was not satisfied with the position and works of the Pharisees. He had been studying the Scriptures with a desire to learn their real meaning. He had a vital interest in the matter, and had asked in sincerity, "What shall I do?" In his answer as to the requirements of the law, he passed by all the mass of ceremonial and ritualistic precepts. For these he claimed no value, but presented the two great principles on which hang all the law and the prophets. This answer, being commended by Christ, placed the Saviour on vantage ground with the rabbis. They could not condemn Him for sanctioning that which had been advanced by an expositor of the law.

"This do, and thou shalt live," Jesus said. He presented the law as a divine unity, and in this lesson taught that it is not possible to keep one precept, and break another; for the same principle runs through them all. Man's destiny will be determined by his obedience to the whole law. Supreme love to God and impartial love to man are the principles to be wrought out in the life.

The lawyer found himself a lawbreaker. He was convicted under Christ's searching words. The righteousness of the law, which he claimed to understand, he had not practiced. He had not manifested love toward his fellow man. Repentance was demanded; but instead of repenting, he tried to justify himself. Rather than acknowledge the truth, he sought to show how difficult of fulfillment the commandment is. Thus he hoped both to parry conviction and to vindicate himself in the eyes of the people. The Saviour's words had shown that his question was needless, since he had been able to answer it himself. Yet he put another question, saying, "Who is my neighbor?"

Among the Jews this question caused endless dispute. They had no doubt as to the heathen and the Samaritans; these were strangers and enemies. But where should the distinction be made among the people of their own nation, and among the different classes of society? Whom should the priest, the rabbi, the elder, regard as neighbor? They spent their lives in a round of ceremonies to make themselves pure. Contact with the ignorant and careless multitude, they taught, would cause defilement that would require wearisome effort to remove. Were they to regard the "unclean" as neighbors?

Again Jesus refused to be drawn into controversy. He did not denounce the bigotry of those who were watching to condemn Him. But by a simple story He held up before His hearers such a picture of the outflowing of heaven-born love as touched all hearts, and drew from the lawyer a confession of the truth.

The way to dispel darkness is to admit light. The best way to deal with error is to present truth. It is the revelation of God's love that makes manifest the deformity and sin of the heart centered in self.

"A certain man," said Jesus, "was going down from Jerusalem to Jericho; and he fell among robbers, which both stripped him and beat him, and departed, leaving him half dead. And by chance a certain priest was going down that way: and when he saw him, he passed by on the other side. And in like manner a Levite also, when he came to the place, and saw him, passed by on the other side." Luke 10:30-32, R.V. This was no imaginary scene, but an actual occurrence, which was known to be exactly as represented. The priest and the Levite who had passed by on the other side were in the company that listened to Christ's words.

In journeying from Jerusalem to Jericho, the traveler had to pass through a portion of the wilderness of Judea. The road led down a wild, rocky ravine, which was infested by robbers, and was often the scene of violence. It was here that the traveler was attacked, stripped of all that was valuable, wounded and bruised, and left half dead by the wayside. As he lay thus, the priest came that way; but he merely glanced toward the wounded man. Then the Levite appeared. Curious to know what had happened, he stopped and looked at the sufferer. He was convicted of what he ought to do; but it was not an agreeable duty. He wished that he had not come that way, so that he need not have seen the wounded man. He persuaded himself that the case was no concern of his.

Both these men were in sacred office, and professed to expound the Scriptures. They were of the class specially chosen to be representatives of God to the people. They were to "have compassion on the ignorant, and on them that are out of the way" (Heb. 5:2), that they might lead men to understand God's great love toward humanity. The work they were called to do was the same that Jesus had described as His own when He said, "The Spirit of the Lord is upon Me, because He hath anointed Me to preach the gospel to the poor; He hath sent Me to heal the brokenhearted, to preach deliverance to the captives, and recovering of sight to the blind, to set at liberty them that are bruised." Luke 4:18.

The angels of heaven look upon the distress of God's family upon the earth, and they are prepared to co-operate with men in relieving oppression and suffering. God in His providence had brought the priest and the Levite along the road where the wounded sufferer lay, that they might see his need of mercy and help. All heaven watched to see if the hearts of these men would be touched with pity for human woe. The Saviour was the One who had instructed the Hebrews in the wilderness; from the pillar of cloud and of fire He had taught a very different lesson from that which the people were now receiving from their priests and teachers. The merciful provisions of the law extended even to the lower animals, which cannot express in words their want and suffering. Directions had been given to Moses for the children of Israel to this effect: "If thou meet thine enemy's ox or his ass going astray, thou shalt surely bring it back to him again. If thou see the ass of him that hateth thee lying under his burden, and wouldest forbear to help him, thou shalt surely help with him." Ex. 23:4, 5. But in the man wounded by robbers, Jesus presented the case of a brother in suffering. How much more should their hearts have been moved with pity for him than for a beast of burden! The message had been given them through Moses that the Lord their God, "a great God, a mighty, and a terrible," "doth execute the judgment of the fatherless and widow, and loveth the stranger." Wherefore He commanded, "Love ye therefore the stranger." "Thou shalt love him as thyself." Deut. 10:17-19; Lev. 19:34.

Job had said, "The stranger did not lodge in the street: but I opened my doors to the traveler." And when the two angels in the guise of men came to Sodom, Lot bowed himself with his face toward the ground, and said, "Behold now, my lords, turn in, I pray you, into your servant's house, and tarry all night." Job 31:32; Gen. 19:2. With all these lessons the priest and the Levite were familiar, but they had not brought them into practical life. Trained in the school of national bigotry, they had become selfish, narrow, and exclusive. When they looked upon the wounded man, they could not tell whether he was of their nation or not. They thought he might be of the Samaritans, and they turned away.

In their action, as Christ had described it, the lawyer saw nothing contrary to what he had been taught concerning the requirements of the law. But now another scene was presented:

A certain Samaritan, in his journey, came where the sufferer was, and when he saw him, he had compassion on him. He did not question whether the stranger was a Jew or a Gentile. If a Jew, the Samaritan well knew that, were their condition reversed, the man would spit in his face, and pass him by with contempt. But he did not hesitate on account of this. He did not consider that he himself might be in danger of violence by tarrying in the place. It was enough that there was before him a human being in need and suffering. He took off his own garment with which to cover him. The oil and wine provided for his own journey he used to heal and refresh the wounded man. He lifted him on his own beast, and moved slowly along with even pace, so that the stranger might not be jarred, and made to suffer increased pain. He brought him to an inn, and cared for him through the night, watching him tenderly. In the morning, as the sick man had improved, the Samaritan ventured to go on his way. But before doing this, he placed him in the care of the innkeeper, paid the charges, and left a deposit for his benefit; and not satisfied even with this, he made provision for any further need, saying to the host, "Take care of him; and whatsoever thou spendest more, when I come again, I will repay thee."

The story ended, Jesus fixed His eyes upon the lawyer, in a glance that seemed to read his soul, and said, "Which of these three, thinkest *thou*, proved neighbor unto him that fell among the robbers?" Luke 10:36, R. V.

The lawyer would not, even now, take the name Samaritan upon his lips, and he made answer, "He that showed mercy on him." Jesus said, "Go, and do *thou* likewise."

Thus the question, "Who is my neighbor?" is forever answered. Christ has shown that our neighbor does not mean merely one of the church or faith to which we belong. It has no reference to race, color, or class distinction. Our neighbor is every person who needs our help. Our neighbor is every soul who is wounded and bruised by the adversary. Our neighbor is everyone who is the property of God.

In the story of the good Samaritan, Jesus gave a picture of Himself and His mission. Man had been deceived, bruised, robbed, and ruined by Satan, and left to perish; but the Saviour had compassion on our helpless condition. He left His glory, to come to our rescue. He found us ready to die, and He undertook our case. He healed our wounds. He covered us with His robe of righteousness. He opened to us a refuge of safety, and made complete provision for us at His own charges. He died to redeem us. Pointing to His own example, He says to His followers, "These things I command you, that ye love one another." "As I have loved you, that ye also love one another." John 15:17; 13:34.

The lawyer's question to Jesus had been, "What shall I do?" And Jesus, recognizing love to God and man as the sum of righteousness, had said, "This do, and thou shalt live." The Samaritan had obeyed the dictates of a kind and loving heart, and in this had proved himself a doer of the law. Christ bade the lawyer, "Go, and do thou likewise." Doing, and not saying merely, is expected of the children of God. "He that saith he abideth in Him ought himself also so to walk, even as He walked." 1 John 2:6.

The lesson is no less needed in the world today than when it fell from the lips of Jesus. Selfishness and cold formality have well-nigh extinguished the fire of love, and dispelled the graces that should make fragrant the character. Many who profess His name have lost sight of the fact that Christians are to represent Christ. Unless there is practical self-sacrifice for the good of others, in the family circle, in the neighborhood, in the church, and wherever we may be, then whatever our profession, we are not Christians.

Christ has linked His interest with that of humanity, and He asks us to become one with Him for the saving of humanity. "Freely ye have received," He says, "freely give." Matt. 10:8. Sin is the greatest of all evils, and it is ours to pity and help the sinner. There are many who err, and who feel their shame and their folly. They are hungry for words of encouragement. They look upon their mistakes and errors, until they are driven almost to desperation. These souls we are not to neglect. If we are Christians, we shall not pass by on the other side, keeping as far as possible from the very ones who most need our help. When we see human beings in distress, whether through affliction or through sin, we shall never say, This does not concern me.

"Ye which are spiritual, restore such an one in the spirit of meekness." Gal. 6:1. By faith and prayer press back the power of the enemy. Speak words of faith and courage that will be as a healing balsam to the bruised and wounded one. Many, many, have fainted and become discouraged in the great struggle of life, when one word of kindly cheer would have strengthened them to overcome. Never should we pass by one suffering soul without seeking to impart to him of the comfort wherewith we are comforted of God.

All this is but a fulfillment of the principle of the law,—the principle that is illustrated in the story of the good Samaritan, and made manifest in the life of Jesus. His character reveals the true significance of the law, and shows what is meant by loving our neighbor as ourselves. And when the children of God manifest mercy, kindness, and love toward all men, they also are witnessing to the character of the statutes of heaven. They are bearing testimony to the fact that "the law of the Lord is perfect, converting the soul." Ps. 19:7. And whoever fails to manifest this love is breaking the law which he professes to revere. For the spirit we manifest toward our brethren declares what is our spirit toward God. The love of God in the heart is the only spring of love toward our neighbor. "If a man say, I love God, and hateth his brother, he is a liar: for he that loveth not his brother whom he hath seen, how can he love God whom he hath not seen?" Beloved, "if we love one another, God dwelleth in us, and His love is perfected in us." 1 John 4:20, 12.

2

Not With Outward Show

This chapter is based on Luke 17:20-22.

Some of the Pharisees had come to Jesus demanding "when the kingdom of God should come." More than three years had passed since John the Baptist gave the message that like a trumpet call had sounded through the land, "The kingdom of heaven is at hand." Matt. 3:2. And as yet these Pharisees saw no indication of the establishment of the kingdom. Many of those who rejected John, and at every step had opposed Jesus, were insinuating that His mission had failed.

Jesus answered, "The kingdom of God cometh not with outward show; [margin]: neither shall they say, Lo here! or, lo there! for, behold, the kingdom of God is within you." The kingdom of God begins in the heart. Look not here or there for manifestations of earthly power to mark its coming.

"The days will come," He said, turning to His disciples, "when ye shall desire to see one of the days of the Son of man, and ye shall not see it." Because it is not attended by worldly pomp, you are in danger of failing to discern the glory of My mission. You do not realize how great is your present privilege in having among you, though veiled in humanity, Him who is the life and the light of men. The days will come when you will look back with longing upon the opportunities you now enjoy to walk and talk with the Son of God.

Because of their selfishness and earthliness, even the disciples of Jesus could not comprehend the spiritual glory which He sought to reveal unto them. It was not until after Christ's ascension to His Father, and the outpouring of the Holy Spirit upon the believers, that the disciples fully appreciated the Saviour's character and mission. After they had received the baptism of the Spirit, they began to realize that they had been in the very presence of the Lord of glory. As the sayings of Christ were brought to their remembrance, their minds were opened to comprehend the prophecies, and to understand the miracles which He had wrought. The wonders of His life passed before them, and they were as men awakened from a dream. They realized that "the Word was made flesh, and dwelt among us, (and we beheld His glory, the glory as of the Only-begotten of the Father,) full of grace and truth." John 1:14. Christ had actually come from God to a sinful world to save the fallen sons and daughters of Adam. The disciples now seemed, to themselves, of much less importance than before they realized this. They never wearied of rehearsing His words and works. His lessons, which they had but dimly understood, now came to them as a fresh revelation. The Scriptures became to them a new book.

As the disciples searched the prophecies that testified of Christ, they were brought into fellowship with the Deity, and learned of Him who had ascended to heaven to complete the work He had begun on earth. They recognized the fact that in Him dwelt knowledge which no human being, unaided by divine agency, could comprehend. They needed the help of Him whom kings, prophets, and righteous men had foretold. With amazement they read and reread the prophetic delineations of His character and work. How dimly had they comprehended the prophetic scriptures! how slow they had been in taking in the great truths which testified of Christ! Looking upon Him in His humiliation, as He walked a man among men, they had not understood the mystery of His incarnation, the dual character of His nature. Their eyes were holden, so that they did not fully recognize divinity in humanity. But after they were illuminated by the Holy Spirit, how they longed to see Him again, and to place themselves at His feet! How they wished that they might come to Him, and have Him explain the scriptures which they could not comprehend! How attentively would they listen to His words! What had Christ meant when He said, "I have yet many things to say unto you, but ye cannot bear them now"? John 16:12. How eager they were to know it all! They grieved that their faith had been so feeble, that their ideas had been so wide of the mark, that they had so failed of comprehending the reality.

A herald had been sent from God to proclaim the coming of Christ, and to call the attention of the Jewish nation and of the world to His mission, that men might prepare for His reception. The wonderful personage whom John had announced had been among them for more than thirty years, and they had not really known Him as the One sent from God. Remorse took hold of the disciples because they had allowed the prevailing unbelief to leaven their opinions and becloud their understanding. The Light of this dark world had been shining amid its gloom, and they had failed to comprehend whence were its beams. They asked themselves why they had pursued a course that made it necessary for Christ to reprove them. They often repeated His conversations, and said, Why did we allow earthly considerations and the opposition of priests and rabbis to confuse our senses, so that we did not comprehend that a greater than Moses was among us, that One wiser than Solomon was instructing us? How dull were our ears! how feeble was our understanding!

Thomas would not believe until he had thrust his finger into the wound made by the Roman soldiers. Peter had denied Him in His humiliation and rejection. These painful remembrances came before them in distinct lines. They had been with Him, but they had not known or appreciated Him. But how these things now stirred their hearts as they recognized their unbelief!

As priests and rulers combined against them, and they were brought before councils and thrust into prison, the followers of Christ rejoiced "that they were counted worthy to suffer shame for His name." Acts 5:41. They rejoiced to prove, before men and angels, that they recognized the glory of Christ, and chose to follow Him at the loss of all things.

It is as true now as in apostolic days, that without the illumination of the divine Spirit, humanity cannot discern the glory of Christ. The truth and the work of God are unappreciated by a world-loving and compromising Christianity. Not in the ways of ease, of earthly honor or worldly conformity, are the followers of the Master found. They are far in advance, in the paths of toil, and humiliation, and reproach, in the front of the battle "against the principalities, against the powers, against the world rulers of this darkness, against the spiritual hosts of wickedness in the heavenly places." Eph. 6:12, R. V. And now, as in Christ's day, they are misunderstood and reproached and oppressed by the priests and Pharisees of their time.

The kingdom of God comes not with outward show. The gospel of the grace of God, with its spirit of self-abnegation, can never be in harmony with the spirit of the world. The two principles are antagonistic. "The natural man receiveth not the things of the Spirit of God: for they are foolishness unto him: neither can he know them, because they are spiritually discerned." 1 Cor. 2:14.

But today in the religious world there are multitudes who, as they believe, are working for the establishment of the kingdom of Christ as an earthly and temporal dominion. They desire to make our Lord the ruler of the kingdoms of this world, the ruler in its courts and camps, its legislative halls, its palaces and market places. They expect Him to rule through legal enactments, enforced by human authority. Since Christ is not now here in person, they themselves will undertake to act in His stead, to execute the laws of His kingdom. The establishment of such a kingdom is what the Jews desired in the days of Christ. They would have received Jesus, had He been willing to establish a temporal dominion, to enforce what they regarded as the laws of God, and to make them the expositors of His will and the agents of His authority. But He said, "My kingdom is not of this world." John 18:36. He would not accept the earthly throne.

The government under which Jesus lived was corrupt and oppressive; on every hand were crying abuses,—extortion, intolerance, and grinding cruelty. Yet the Saviour attempted no civil reforms. He attacked no national abuses, nor condemned the national enemies. He did not interfere with the authority or administration of those in power. He who was our example kept aloof from earthly governments. Not because He was indifferent to the woes of men, but because the remedy did not lie in merely human and external measures. To be efficient, the cure must reach men individually, and must regenerate the heart.

Not by the decisions of courts or councils or legislative assemblies, not by the patronage of worldly great men, is the kingdom of Christ established, but by the implanting of Christ's nature in humanity through the work of the Holy Spirit. "As many as received Him, to them gave He power to become the sons of God, even to them that believe on His name: which were born, not of blood, nor of the will of the flesh, nor of the will of man, but of God." John 1:12, 13. Here is the only power that can work the uplifting of mankind. And the human agency for the accomplishment of this work is the teaching and practicing of the word of God.

When the apostle Paul began his ministry in Corinth, that populous, wealthy, and wicked city, polluted by the nameless vices of heathenism, he said, "I determined not to know anything among you, save Jesus Christ, and Him crucified." 1 Cor. 2:2. Writing afterward to some of those who had been corrupted by the foulest sins, he could say, "But ye are washed, but ye are sanctified, but ye are justified in the name of the Lord Jesus, and by the Spirit of our God." "I thank my God always on your behalf, for the grace of God which is given you by Jesus Christ." 1 Cor. 6:11; 1:4.

Now, as in Christ's day, the work of God's kingdom lies not with those who are clamoring for recognition and support by earthly rulers and human laws, but with those who are declaring to the people in His name those spiritual truths that will work in the receivers the experience of Paul: "I am crucified with Christ: nevertheless I live; yet not I, but Christ liveth in me." Gal. 2:20. Then they will labor as did Paul for the benefit of men. He said, "Now then we are ambassadors for Christ, as though God did beseech you by us: we pray you in Christ's stead, be ye reconciled to God." 2 Cor. 5:20.

3

Blessing the Children

This chapter is based on Matthew 19:13-15; Mark 10:13-16; Luke 18:15-17.

Jesus was ever a lover of children. He accepted their childish sympathy and their open, unaffected love. The grateful praise from their pure lips was music in His ears, and refreshed His spirit when oppressed by contact with crafty and hypocritical men. Wherever the Saviour went, the benignity of His countenance, and His gentle, kindly manner won the love and confidence of children.

Among the Jews it was customary for children to be brought to some rabbi, that he might lay his hands upon them in blessing; but the Saviour's disciples thought His work too important to be interrupted in this way. When the mothers came to Him with their little ones, the disciples looked on them with disfavor. They thought these children too young to be benefited by a visit to Jesus, and concluded that He would be displeased at their presence. But it was the disciples with whom He was displeased. The Saviour understood the care and burden of the mothers who were seeking to train their children according to the word of God. He had heard their prayers. He Himself had drawn them into His presence.

One mother with her child had left her home to find Jesus. On the way she told a neighbor her errand, and the neighbor wanted to have Jesus bless her children. Thus several mothers came together, with their little ones. Some of the children had passed beyond the years of infancy to childhood and youth. When the mothers made known their desire, Jesus heard with sympathy the timid, tearful request. But He waited to see how the disciples would treat them. When He saw them send the mothers away, thinking to do Him a favor, He showed them their error, saying, "Suffer the little children to come unto Me, and forbid them not: for of such is the kingdom of God." He took the children in His arms, He laid His hands upon them, and gave them the blessing for which they came.

The mothers were comforted. They returned to their homes strengthened and blessed by the words of Christ. They were encouraged to take up their burden with new cheerfulness, and to work hopefully for their children. The mothers of today are to receive His words with the same faith. Christ is as verily a personal Saviour today as when He lived a man among men. He is as verily the helper of mothers today as when He gathered the little ones to His arms in Judea. The children of our hearths are as much the purchase of His blood as were the children of long ago.

Jesus knows the burden of every mother's heart. He who had a mother that struggled with poverty and privation sympathizes with every mother in her labors. He who made a long journey in order to relieve the anxious heart of a Canaanite woman will do as much for the mothers of today. He who gave back to the widow of Nain her only son, and who in His agony upon the cross remembered His own mother, is touched today by the mother's sorrow. In every grief and every need He will give comfort and help.

Let mothers come to Jesus with their perplexities. They will find grace sufficient to aid them in the management of their children. The gates are open for every mother who would lay her burdens at the Saviour's feet. He who said, "Suffer the little children to come unto Me, and forbid them not," still invites the mothers to lead up their little ones to be blessed by Him. Even the babe in its mother's arms may dwell as under the shadow of the Almighty through the faith of the praying mother. John the Baptist was filled with the Holy Spirit from his birth. If we will live in communion with God, we too may expect the divine Spirit to mold our little ones, even from their earliest moments.

In the children who were brought in contact with Him, Jesus saw the men and women who should be heirs of His grace and subjects of His kingdom, and some of whom would become martyrs for His sake. He knew that these children would listen to Him and accept Him as their Redeemer far more readily than would grown-up people, many of whom were the worldly-wise and hardhearted. In His teaching He came down to their level. He, the Majesty of heaven, did not disdain to answer their questions, and simplify His important lessons to meet their childish understanding. He planted in their minds the seeds of truth, which in after years would spring up, and bear fruit unto eternal life.

It is still true that children are the most susceptible to the teachings of the gospel; their hearts are open to divine influences, and strong to retain the lessons received. The little children may be Christians, having an experience in accordance with their years. They need to be educated in spiritual things, and parents should give them every advantage, that they may form characters after the similitude of the character of Christ.

Fathers and mothers should look upon their children as younger members of the Lord's family, committed to them to educate for heaven. The lessons that we ourselves learn from Christ we should give to our children, as the young minds can receive them, little by little opening to them the beauty of the principles of heaven. Thus the Christian home becomes a school, where the parents serve as underteachers, while Christ Himself is the chief instructor.

In working for the conversion of our children, we should not look for violent emotion as the essential evidence of conviction of sin. Nor is it necessary to know the exact time when they are converted. We should teach them to bring their sins to Jesus, asking His forgiveness, and believing that He pardons and receives them as He received the children when He was personally on earth.

As the mother teaches her children to obey her because they love her, she is teaching them the first lessons in the Christian life. The mother's love represents to the child the love of Christ, and the little ones who trust and obey their mother are learning to trust and obey the Saviour.

Jesus was the pattern for children, and He was also the father's example. He spoke as one having authority, and His word was with power; yet in all His intercourse with rude and violent men He did not use one unkind or discourteous expression. The grace of Christ in the heart will impart a heaven-born dignity and sense of propriety. It will soften whatever is harsh, and subdue all that is coarse and unkind. It will lead fathers and mothers to treat their children as intelligent beings, as they themselves would like to be treated.

Parents, in the training of your children, study the lessons that God has given in nature. If you would train a pink, or rose, or lily, how would you do it? Ask the gardener by what process he makes every branch and leaf to flourish so beautifully, and to develop in symmetry and loveliness. He will tell you that it was by no rude touch, no violent effort; for this would only break the delicate stems. It was by little attentions, often repeated. He moistened the soil, and protected the growing plants from the fierce blasts and from the scorching sun, and God caused them to flourish and to blossom into loveliness. In dealing with your children, follow the method of the gardener. By gentle touches, by loving ministrations, seek to fashion their characters after the pattern of the character of Christ.

Encourage the expression of love toward God and toward one another. The reason why there are so many hardhearted men and women in the world is that true affection has been regarded as weakness, and has been discouraged and repressed. The better nature of these persons was stifled in childhood; and unless the light of divine love shall melt away their cold selfishness, their happiness will be forever ruined. If we wish our children to possess the tender spirit of Jesus, and the sympathy that angels manifest for us, we must encourage the generous, loving impulses of childhood.

Teach the children to see Christ in nature. Take them out into the open air, under the noble trees, into the garden; and in all the wonderful works of creation teach them to see an expression of His love. Teach them that He made the laws which govern all living things, that He has made laws for us, and that these laws are for our happiness and joy. Do not weary them with long prayers and tedious exhortations, but through nature's object lessons teach them obedience to the law of God.

As you win their confidence in you as followers of Christ, it will be easy to teach them of the great love wherewith He has loved us. As you try to make plain the truths of salvation, and point the children to Christ as a personal Saviour, angels will be by your side. The Lord will give to fathers and mothers grace to interest their little ones in the precious story of the Babe of Bethlehem, who is indeed the hope of the world.

When Jesus told the disciples not to forbid the children to come to Him, He was speaking to His followers in all ages,—to officers of the church, to ministers, helpers, and all Christians. Jesus is drawing the children, and He bids us, Suffer them to come; as if He would say, They will come if you do not hinder them.

Let not your un-Christlike character misrepresent Jesus. Do not keep the little ones away from Him by your coldness and harshness. Never give them cause to feel that heaven will not be a pleasant place to them if you are there. Do not speak of religion as something that children cannot understand, or act as if they were not expected to accept Christ in their childhood. Do not give them the false impression that the religion of Christ is a religion of gloom, and that in coming to the Saviour they must give up all that makes life joyful.

As the Holy Spirit moves upon the hearts of the children, co-operate with His work. Teach them that the Saviour is calling them, that nothing can give Him greater joy than for them to give themselves to Him in the bloom and freshness of their years.

The Saviour regards with infinite tenderness the souls whom He has purchased with His own blood. They are the claim of His love. He looks upon them with unutterable longing. His heart is drawn out, not only to the best-behaved children, but to those who have by inheritance objectionable traits of character. Many parents do not understand how much they are responsible for these traits in their children. They have not the tenderness and wisdom to deal with the erring ones whom they have made what they are. But Jesus looks upon these children with pity. He traces from cause to effect.

The Christian worker may be Christ's agent in drawing these children to the Saviour. By wisdom and tact he may bind them to his heart, he may give them courage and hope, and through the grace of Christ may see them transformed in character, so that of them it may be said, "Of such is the kingdom of God."

4

"One Thing Thou Lackest"

This chapter is based on Matthew 19:16-22; Mark 10:17-22; Luke 18:18-23.

"And when He was gone forth into the way, there came one running, and kneeled to Him, and asked Him, Good Master, what shall I do that I may inherit eternal life?"

The young man who asked this question was a ruler. He had great possessions, and occupied a position of responsibility. He saw the love that Christ manifested toward the children brought to Him; he saw how tenderly He received them, and took them up in His arms, and his heart kindled with love for the Saviour. He felt a desire to be His disciple. He was so deeply moved that as Christ was going on His way, he ran after Him, and kneeling at His feet, asked with sincerity and earnestness the question so important to his soul and to the soul of every human being, "Good Master, what shall I do that I may inherit eternal life?"

"Why callest thou Me good?" said Christ, "there is none good but One, that is, God." Jesus desired to test the ruler's sincerity, and to draw from him the way in which he regarded Him as good. Did he realize that the One to whom he was speaking was the Son of God? What was the true sentiment of his heart?

This ruler had a high estimate of his own righteousness. He did not really suppose that he was defective in anything, yet he was not altogether satisfied. He felt the want of something that he did not possess. Could not Jesus bless him as He blessed the little children, and satisfy his soul want?

In reply to this question Jesus told him that obedience to the commandments of God was necessary if he would obtain eternal life; and He quoted several of the commandments which show man's duty to his fellow men. The ruler's answer was positive: "All these things have I kept from my youth up: what lack I yet?"

Christ looked into the face of the young man, as if reading his life and searching his character. He loved him, and He hungered to give him that peace and grace and joy which would materially change his character. "One thing thou lackest," He said; "go thy way, sell whatsoever thou hast, and give to the poor, and thou shalt have treasure in heaven: and come, take up the cross, and follow Me."

Christ was drawn to this young man. He knew him to be sincere in his assertion, "All these things have I kept from my youth." The Redeemer longed to create in him that discernment which would enable him to see the necessity of heart devotion and Christian goodness. He longed to see in him a humble and contrite heart, conscious of the supreme love to be given to God, and hiding its lack in the perfection of Christ.

Jesus saw in this ruler just the help He needed if the young man would become a colaborer with Him in the work of salvation. If he would place himself under Christ's guidance, he would be a power for good. In a marked degree the ruler could have represented Christ; for he possessed qualifications, which, if he were united with the Saviour, would enable him to become a divine force among men. Christ, seeing into his character, loved him. Love for Christ was awakening in the ruler's heart; for love begets love. Jesus longed to see him a co-worker with Him. He longed to make him like Himself, a mirror in which the likeness of God would be reflected. He longed to develop the excellence of his character, and sanctify it to the Master's use. If the ruler had then given himself to Christ, he would have grown in the atmosphere of His presence. If he had made this choice, how different would have been his future!

"One thing thou lackest," Jesus said. "If thou wilt be perfect, go and sell that thou hast, and give to the poor, and thou shalt have treasure in heaven: and come and follow Me." Christ read the ruler's heart. Only one thing he lacked, but that was a vital principle. He needed the love of God in the soul. This lack, unless supplied, would prove fatal to him; his whole nature would become corrupted. By indulgence, selfishness would strengthen. That he might receive the love of God, his supreme love of self must be surrendered.

Christ gave this man a test. He called upon him to choose between the heavenly treasure and worldly greatness. The heavenly treasure was assured him if he would follow Christ. But self must yield; his will must be given into Christ's control. The very holiness of God was offered to the young ruler. He had the privilege of becoming a son of God, and a coheir with Christ to the heavenly treasure. But he must take up the cross, and follow the Saviour in the path of self-denial.

Christ's words were verily to the ruler the invitation, "Choose you this day whom ye will serve." Joshua 24:15. The choice was left with him. Jesus was yearning for his conversion. He had shown him the plague spot in his character, and with what deep interest He watched the issue as the young man weighed the question! If he decided to follow Christ, he must obey His words in everything. He must turn from his ambitious projects. With what earnest, anxious longing, what soul hunger, did the Saviour look at the young man, hoping that he would yield to the invitation of the Spirit of God!

Christ made the only terms which could place the ruler where he would perfect a Christian character. His words were words of wisdom, though they appeared severe and exacting. In accepting and obeying them was the ruler's only hope of salvation. His exalted position and his possessions were exerting a subtle influence for evil upon his character. If cherished, they would supplant God in his affections. To keep back little or much from God was to retain that which would lessen his moral strength and efficiency; for if the things of this world are cherished, however uncertain and unworthy they may be, they will become all-absorbing.

The ruler was quick to discern all that Christ's words involved, and he became sad. If he had realized the value of the offered gift, quickly would he have enrolled himself as one of Christ's followers. He was a member of the honored council of the Jews, and Satan was tempting him with flattering prospects of the future. He wanted the heavenly treasure, but he wanted also the temporal advantages his riches would bring him. He was sorry that such conditions existed; he desired eternal life, but he was not willing to make the sacrifice. The cost of eternal life seemed too great, and he went away sorrowful; "for he had great possessions."

His claim that he had kept the law of God was a deception. He showed that riches were his idol. He could not keep the commandments of God while the world was first in his affections. He loved the gifts of God more than he loved the Giver. Christ had offered the young man fellowship with Himself. "Follow Me," He said. But the Saviour was not so much to him as his own name among men or his possessions. To give up his earthly treasure, that was seen, for the heavenly treasure, that was unseen, was too great a risk. He refused the offer of eternal life, and went away, and ever after the world was to receive his worship. Thousands are passing through this ordeal, weighing Christ against the world; and many choose the world. Like the young ruler, they turn from the Saviour, saying in their hearts, I will not have this Man as my leader.

Christ's dealing with the young man is presented as an object lesson. God has given us the rule of conduct which every one of His servants must follow. It is obedience to His law, not merely a legal obedience, but an obedience which enters into the life, and is exemplified in the character. God has set His own standard of character for all who would become subjects of His kingdom. Only those who will become co-workers with Christ, only those who will say, Lord, all I have and all I am is Thine, will be acknowledged as sons and daughters of God. All should consider what it means to desire heaven, and yet to turn away because of the conditions laid down. Think of what it means to say "No" to Christ. The ruler said, No, I cannot give You all. Do we say the same? The Saviour offers to share with us the work God has given us to do. He offers to use the means God has given us, to carry forward His work in the world. Only in this way can He save us.

The ruler's possessions were entrusted to him that he might prove himself a faithful steward; he was to dispense these goods for the blessing of those in need. So God now entrusts men with means, with talents and opportunities, that they may be His agents in helping the poor and the suffering. He who uses his entrusted gifts as God designs becomes a co-worker with the Saviour. He wins souls to Christ, because he is a representative of His character.

To those who, like the young ruler, are in high positions of trust and have great possessions, it may seem too great a sacrifice to give up all in order to follow Christ. But this is the rule of conduct for all who would become His disciples. Nothing short of obedience can be accepted. Self-surrender is the substance of the teachings of Christ. Often it is presented and enjoined in language that seems authoritative, because there is no other way to save man than to cut away those things which, if entertained, will demoralize the whole being.

When Christ's followers give back to the Lord His own, they are accumulating treasure which will be given to them when they shall hear the words, "Well done, good and faithful servant; ... enter thou into the joy of thy Lord." "Who for the joy that was set before Him endured the cross, despising the shame, and is set down at the right hand of the throne of God." Matt. 25:23; Heb. 12:2. The joy of seeing souls redeemed, souls eternally saved, is the reward of all that put their feet in the footprints of Him who said, "Follow Me."

5

"Lazarus, Come Forth"

This chapter is based on Luke 10:38-42; John 11:1-44.

Among the most steadfast of Christ's disciples was Lazarus of Bethany. From their first meeting his faith in Christ had been strong; his love for Him was deep, and he was greatly beloved by the Saviour. It was for Lazarus that the greatest of Christ's miracles was performed. The Saviour blessed all who sought His help; He loves all the human family, but to some He is bound by peculiarly tender associations. His heart was knit by a strong bond of affection to the family at Bethany, and for one of them His most wonderful work was wrought.

At the home of Lazarus, Jesus had often found rest. The Saviour had no home of His own; He was dependent on the hospitality of His friends and disciples, and often, when weary, thirsting for human fellowship, He had been glad to escape to this peaceful household, away from the suspicion and jealousy of the angry Pharisees. Here He found a sincere welcome, and pure, holy friendship. Here He could speak with simplicity and perfect freedom, knowing that His words would be understood and treasured.

Our Saviour appreciated a quiet home and interested listeners. He longed for human tenderness, courtesy, and affection. Those who received the heavenly instruction He was always ready to impart were greatly blessed. As the multitudes followed Christ through the open fields, He unfolded to them the beauties of the natural world. He sought to open the eyes of their understanding, that they might see how the hand of God upholds the world. In order to call out an appreciation of God's goodness and benevolence, He called the attention of His hearers to the gently falling dew, to the soft showers of rain and the bright sunshine, given alike to good and evil. He desired men to realize more fully the regard that God bestows on the human instrumentalities He has created. But the multitudes were slow of hearing, and in the home at Bethany Christ found rest from the weary conflict of public life. Here He opened to an appreciative audience the volume of Providence. In these private interviews He unfolded to His hearers that which He did not attempt to tell to the mixed multitude. He needed not to speak to His friends in parables.

As Christ gave His wonderful lessons, Mary sat at His feet, a reverent and devoted listener. On one occasion, Martha, perplexed with the care of preparing the meal, went to Christ, saying, "Lord, dost Thou not care that

my sister hath left me to serve alone? bid her therefore that she help me."
This was the time of Christ's first visit to Bethany. The Saviour and His
disciples had just made the toilsome journey on foot from Jericho. Martha
was anxious to provide for their comfort, and in her anxiety she forgot
the courtesy due to her Guest. Jesus answered her with mild and patient
words, "Martha, Martha, thou art careful and troubled about many things:
but one thing is needful: and Mary hath chosen that good part, which shall
not be taken away from her." Mary was storing her mind with the precious
words falling from the Saviour's lips, words that were more precious to
her than earth's most costly jewels.

The "one thing" that Martha needed was a calm, devotional spirit, a
deeper anxiety for knowledge concerning the future, immortal life, and
the graces necessary for spiritual advancement. She needed less anxiety
for the things which pass away, and more for those things which endure
forever. Jesus would teach His children to seize every opportunity of gaining that knowledge which will make them wise unto salvation. The cause
of Christ needs careful, energetic workers. There is a wide field for the
Marthas, with their zeal in active religious work. But let them first sit with
Mary at the feet of Jesus. Let diligence, promptness, and energy be sanctified by the grace of Christ; then the life will be an unconquerable power
for good.

Sorrow entered the peaceful home where Jesus had rested. Lazarus
was stricken with sudden illness, and his sisters sent to the Saviour, saying,
"Lord, behold, he whom Thou lovest is sick." They saw the violence of
the disease that had seized their brother, but they knew that Christ had
shown Himself able to heal all manner of diseases. They believed that
He would sympathize with them in their distress; therefore they made no
urgent demand for His immediate presence, but sent only the confiding
message, "He whom Thou lovest is sick." They thought that He would
·immediately respond to their message, and be with them as soon as He
could reach Bethany.

Anxiously they waited for a word from Jesus. As long as the spark
of life was yet alive in their brother, they prayed and watched for Jesus
to come. But the messenger returned without Him. Yet he brought the
message, "This sickness is not unto death," and they clung to the hope
that Lazarus would live. Tenderly they tried to speak words of hope and
encouragement to the almost unconscious sufferer. When Lazarus died,
they were bitterly disappointed; but they felt the sustaining grace of Christ,
and this kept them from reflecting any blame on the Saviour.

When Christ heard the message, the disciples thought He received
it coldly. He did not manifest the sorrow they expected Him to show.

Looking up to them, He said, "This sickness is not unto death, but for the glory of God, that the Son of God might be glorified thereby." For two days He remained in the place where He was. This delay was a mystery to the disciples. What a comfort His presence would be to the afflicted household! they thought. His strong affection for the family at Bethany was well known to the disciples, and they were surprised that He did not respond to the sad message, "He whom Thou lovest is sick."

During the two days Christ seemed to have dismissed the message from His mind; for He did not speak of Lazarus. The disciples thought of John the Baptist, the forerunner of Jesus. They had wondered why Jesus, with the power to perform wonderful miracles, had permitted John to languish in prison, and to die a violent death. Possessing such power, why did not Christ save John's life? This question had often been asked by the Pharisees, who presented it as an unanswerable argument against Christ's claim to be the Son of God. The Saviour had warned His disciples of trials, losses, and persecution. Would He forsake them in trial? Some questioned if they had mistaken His mission. All were deeply troubled.

After waiting for two days, Jesus said to the disciples, "Let us go into Judea again." The disciples questioned why, if Jesus were going to Judea, He had waited two days. But anxiety for Christ and for themselves was now uppermost in their minds. They could see nothing but danger in the course He was about to pursue. "Master," they said, "the Jews of late sought to stone Thee; and goest Thou thither again? Jesus answered, Are there not twelve hours in the day?" I am under the guidance of My Father; as long as I do His will, My life is safe. My twelve hours of day are not yet ended. I have entered upon the last remnant of My day; but while any of this remains, I am safe.

"If any man walk in the day," He continued, "he stumbleth not, because he seeth the light of this world." He who does the will of God, who walks in the path that God has marked out, cannot stumble and fall. The light of God's guiding Spirit gives him a clear perception of his duty, and leads him aright till the close of his work. "But if a man walk in the night, he stumbleth, because there is no light in him." He who walks in a path of his own choosing, where God has not called him, will stumble. For him day is turned into night, and wherever he may be, he is not secure.

"These things said He: and after that He saith unto them, Our friend Lazarus sleepeth; but I go that I may awake him out of sleep." "Our friend Lazarus sleepeth." How touching the words! how full of sympathy! In the thought of the peril their Master was about to incur by going to Jerusalem, the disciples had almost forgotten the bereaved family at Bethany. But not so Christ. The disciples felt rebuked. They had been disappointed because

Christ did not respond more promptly to the message. They had been tempted to think that He had not the tender love for Lazarus and his sisters that they had thought He had, or He would have hastened back with the messenger. But the words, "Our friend Lazarus sleepeth," awakened right feelings in their minds. They were convinced that Christ had not forgotten His suffering friends.

"Then said His disciples, Lord, if he sleep, he shall do well. Howbeit Jesus spake of his death: but they thought that He had spoken of taking of rest in sleep." Christ represents death as a sleep to His believing children. Their life is hid with Christ in God, and until the last trump shall sound those who die will sleep in Him.

"Then said Jesus unto them plainly, Lazarus is dead. And I am glad for your sakes that I was not there, to the intent ye may believe; nevertheless let us go unto him." Thomas could see nothing but death in store for his Master if he went to Judea; but he girded up his spirit, and said to the other disciples, "Let us also go, that we may die with Him." He knew the hatred of the Jews toward Christ. It was their purpose to compass His death, but this purpose had not succeeded, because some of His allotted time still remained. During this time Jesus had the guardianship of heavenly angels; and even in the regions of Judea, where the rabbis were plotting how they might take Him and put Him to death, no harm could come to Him.

The disciples marveled at Christ's words when He said, "Lazarus is dead. And I am glad … that I was not there." Did the Saviour by His own choice avoid the home of His suffering friends? Apparently Mary and Martha and the dying Lazarus were left alone. But they were not alone. Christ beheld the whole scene, and after the death of Lazarus the bereaved sisters were upheld by His grace. Jesus witnessed the sorrow of their rent hearts, as their brother wrestled with his strong foe, death. He felt every pang of anguish, as He said to His disciples, "Lazarus is dead." But Christ had not only the loved ones at Bethany to think of; He had the training of His disciples to consider. They were to be His representatives to the world, that the Father's blessing might embrace all. For their sake He permitted Lazarus to die. Had He restored him from illness to health, the miracle that is the most positive evidence of His divine character, would not have been performed.

Had Christ been in the sickroom, Lazarus would not have died; for Satan would have had no power over him. Death could not have aimed his dart at Lazarus in the presence of the Life-giver. Therefore Christ remained away. He suffered the enemy to exercise his power, that He might drive him back, a conquered foe. He permitted Lazarus to pass under the dominion of death; and the suffering sisters saw their brother laid in the grave. Christ knew that as they looked on the dead face of their brother their faith in their Redeemer would be severely tried. But He knew that because of the struggle through which they were now passing their faith would shine forth with far greater power. He suffered every pang of sorrow that they endured. He loved them no less because He tarried; but He knew that for them, for Lazarus, for Himself, and for His disciples, a victory was to be gained.

"For your sakes," "to the intent ye may believe." To all who are reaching out to feel the guiding hand of God, the moment of greatest discouragement is the time when divine help is nearest. They will look back with thankfulness upon the darkest part of their way. "The Lord knoweth how to deliver the godly," 2 Peter 2:9. From every temptation and every trial He will bring them forth with firmer faith and a richer experience.

In delaying to come to Lazarus, Christ had a purpose of mercy toward those who had not received Him. He tarried, that by raising Lazarus from the dead He might give to His stubborn, unbelieving people another evidence that He was indeed "the resurrection, and the life." He was loath to give up all hope of the people, the poor, wandering sheep of the house of Israel. His heart was breaking because of their impenitence. In His mercy He purposed to give them one more evidence that He was the Restorer, the One who alone could bring life and immortality to light. This was to be an evidence that the priests could not misinterpret. This was the reason of His delay in going to Bethany. This crowning miracle, the raising of Lazarus, was to set the seal of God on His work and on His claim to divinity.

On His journey to Bethany, Jesus, according to His custom, ministered to the sick and the needy. Upon reaching the town He sent a messenger to the sisters with the tidings of His arrival. Christ did not at once enter the house, but remained in a quiet place by the wayside. The great outward display observed by the Jews at the death of friends or relatives was not in harmony with the spirit of Christ. He heard the sound of wailing from the hired mourners, and He did not wish to meet the sisters in the scene of confusion. Among the mourning friends were relatives of the family, some of whom held high positions of responsibility in Jerusalem. Among these were some of Christ's bitterest enemies. Christ knew their purposes, and therefore He did not at once make Himself known.

The message was given to Martha so quietly that others in the room did not hear. Absorbed in her grief, Mary did not hear the words. Rising at once, Martha went out to meet her Lord, but thinking that she had gone to the place where Lazarus was buried, Mary sat still in her sorrow, making no outcry.

Martha hastened to meet Jesus, her heart agitated by conflicting emotions. In His expressive face she read the same tenderness and love that had always been there. Her confidence in Him was unbroken, but she thought of her dearly loved brother, whom Jesus also had loved. With grief surging in her heart because Christ had not come before, yet with hope that even now He would do something to comfort them, she said, "Lord, if Thou hadst been here, my brother had not died." Over and over again, amid the tumult made by the mourners, the sisters had repeated these words.

With human and divine pity Jesus looked into her sorrowful, careworn face. Martha had no inclination to recount the past; all was expressed by the pathetic words, "Lord, if Thou hadst been here, my brother had not died." But looking into that face of love, she added, "I know, that even now, whatsoever Thou wilt ask of God, God will give it Thee."

Jesus encouraged her faith, saying, "Thy brother shall rise again." His answer was not intended to inspire hope of an immediate change. He carried Martha's thoughts beyond the present restoration of her brother, and fixed them upon the resurrection of the just. This He did that she might see in the resurrection of Lazarus a pledge of the resurrection of all the righteous dead, and an assurance that it would be accomplished by the Saviour's power.

Martha answered, "I know that he shall rise again in the resurrection at the last day."

Still seeking to give a true direction to her faith, Jesus declared, "I am the resurrection, and the life." In Christ is life, original, unborrowed, underived. "He that hath the Son hath life." 1 John 5:12. The divinity of Christ is the believer's assurance of eternal life. "He that believeth in Me," said Jesus, "though he were dead, yet shall he live: and whosoever liveth and believeth in Me shall never die. Believest thou this?" Christ here looks forward to the time of His second coming. Then the righteous dead shall be raised incorruptible, and the living righteous shall be translated to heaven without seeing death. The miracle which Christ was about to perform, in raising Lazarus from the dead, would represent the resurrection of all the righteous dead. By His word and His works He declared Himself the Author of the resurrection. He who Himself was soon to die upon the cross stood with the keys of death, a conqueror of the grave, and asserted His right and power to give eternal life.

To the Saviour's words, "Believest thou?" Martha responded, "Yea, Lord: I believe that Thou art the Christ, the Son of God, which should come into the world." She did not comprehend in all their significance the words spoken by Christ, but she confessed her faith in His divinity, and her confidence that He was able to perform whatever it pleased Him to do.

"And when she had so said, she went her way, and called Mary her sister secretly, saying, The Master is come, and calleth for thee." She delivered her message as quietly as possible; for the priests and rulers were prepared to arrest Jesus when opportunity offered. The cries of the mourners prevented her words from being heard.

On hearing the message, Mary rose hastily, and with an eager look on her face left the room. Thinking that she had gone to the grave to weep, the mourners followed her. When she reached the place where Jesus was waiting, she knelt at His feet, and said with quivering lips, "Lord, if Thou hadst been here, my brother had not died." The cries of the mourners were painful to her; for she longed for a few quiet words alone with Jesus. But she knew of the envy and jealousy cherished in the hearts of some present against Christ, and she was restrained from fully expressing her grief.

"When Jesus therefore saw her weeping, and the Jews also weeping which came with her, He groaned in the spirit, and was troubled." He read the hearts of all assembled. He saw that with many, what passed as a demonstration of grief was only pretense. He knew that some in the company, now manifesting hypocritical sorrow, would erelong be planning the death, not only of the mighty miracle worker, but of the one to be raised from the dead. Christ could have stripped from them their robe of pretended sorrow. But He restrained His righteous indignation. The words He could in all truth have spoken, He did not speak, because of the loved one kneeling at His feet in sorrow, who truly believed in Him.

"Where have ye laid him?" He asked, "They said unto Him, Lord, come and see." Together they proceeded to the grave. It was a mournful scene. Lazarus had been much beloved, and his sisters wept for him with breaking hearts, while those who had been his friends mingled their tears with those of the bereaved sisters. In view of this human distress, and of the fact that the afflicted friends could mourn over the dead while the Saviour of the world stood by,—"Jesus wept." Though He was the Son of God, yet He had taken human nature upon Him, and He was moved by human sorrow. His tender, pitying heart is ever awakened to sympathy by suffering. He weeps with those that weep, and rejoices with those that rejoice.

But it was not only because of His human sympathy with Mary and Martha that Jesus wept. In His tears there was a sorrow as high above human sorrow as the heavens are higher than the earth. Christ did not weep for Lazarus; for He was about to call him from the grave. He wept because many of those now mourning for Lazarus would soon plan the death of Him who was the resurrection and the life. But how unable were the unbelieving Jews rightly to interpret His tears! Some, who could see nothing more than the outward circumstances of the scene before Him as a cause for His grief, said softly, "Behold how He loved him!" Others, seeking to drop the seed of unbelief into the hearts of those present, said derisively,

"Could not this Man, which opened the eyes of the blind, have caused that even this man should not have died?" If it were in Christ's power to save Lazarus, why then did He suffer him to die?

With prophetic eye Christ saw the enmity of the Pharisees and the Sadducees. He knew that they were premeditating His death. He knew that some of those now apparently so sympathetic would soon close against themselves the door of hope and the gates of the city of God. A scene was about to take place, in His humiliation and crucifixion, that would result in the destruction of Jerusalem, and at that time none would make lamentation for the dead. The retribution that was coming upon Jerusalem was plainly portrayed before Him. He saw Jerusalem compassed by the Roman legions. He knew that many now weeping for Lazarus would die in the siege of the city, and in their death there would be no hope.

It was not only because of the scene before Him that Christ wept. The weight of the grief of ages was upon Him. He saw the terrible effects of the transgression of God's law. He saw that in the history of the world, beginning with the death of Abel, the conflict between good and evil had been unceasing. Looking down the years to come, He saw the suffering and sorrow, tears and death, that were to be the lot of men. His heart was pierced with the pain of the human family of all ages and in all lands. The woes of the sinful race were heavy upon His soul, and the fountain of His tears was broken up as He longed to relieve all their distress.

"Jesus therefore again groaning in Himself cometh to the grave." Lazarus had been laid in a cave in a rock, and a massive stone had been placed before the entrance. "Take ye away the stone," Christ said. Thinking that He only wished to look upon the dead, Martha objected, saying that the body had been buried four days, and corruption had already begun its work. This statement, made before the raising of Lazarus, left no room for Christ's enemies to say that a deception had been practiced. In the past the Pharisees had circulated false statements regarding the most wonderful manifestations of the power of God. When Christ raised to life the daughter of Jairus, He had said, "The damsel is not dead, but sleepeth." Mark 5:39. As she had been sick only a short time, and was raised immediately after death, the Pharisees declared that the child had not been dead; that Christ Himself had said she was only asleep. They had tried to make it appear that Christ could not cure disease, that there was foul play about His miracles. But in this case, none could deny that Lazarus was dead.

When the Lord is about to do a work, Satan moves upon someone to object. "Take ye away the stone," Christ said. As far as possible, prepare the way for My work. But Martha's positive and ambitious nature asserted itself. She was unwilling that the decomposing body should be brought to view. The human heart is slow to understand Christ's words, and Martha's faith had not grasped the true meaning of His promise.

Christ reproved Martha, but His words were spoken with the utmost gentleness. "Said I not unto thee, that, if thou wouldest believe, thou shouldest see the glory of God?" Why should you doubt in regard to My power? Why reason in opposition to My requirements? You have My word. If you will believe, you shall see the glory of God. Natural impossibilities cannot prevent the work of the Omnipotent One. Skepticism and unbelief are not humility. Implicit belief in Christ's word is true humility, true self-surrender.

"Take *ye* away the stone." Christ could have commanded the stone to remove, and it would have obeyed His voice. He could have bidden the angels who were close by His side to do this. At His bidding, invisible hands would have removed the stone. But it was to be taken away by human hands. Thus Christ would show that humanity is to co-operate with divinity. What human power can do divine power is not summoned to do. God does not dispense with man's aid. He strengthens him, co-operating with him as he uses the powers and capabilities given him.

The command is obeyed. The stone is rolled away. Everything is done openly and deliberately. All are given a chance to see that no deception is practiced. There lies the body of Lazarus in its rocky grave, cold and silent in death. The cries of the mourners are hushed. Surprised and expectant, the company stand around the sepulcher, waiting to see what is to follow.

Calmly Christ stands before the tomb. A sacred solemnity rests upon all present. Christ steps closer to the sepulcher. Lifting His eyes to heaven, He says, "Father, I thank Thee that Thou hast heard Me." Not long before this, Christ's enemies had accused Him of blasphemy, and had taken up stones to cast at Him because He claimed to be the Son of God. They accused Him of performing miracles by the power of Satan. But here Christ claims God as His Father, and with perfect confidence declares that He is the Son of God.

In all that He did, Christ was co-operating with His Father. Ever He had been careful to make it evident that He did not work independently; it was by faith and prayer that He wrought His miracles. Christ desired all to know His relationship with His Father. "Father," He said, "I thank Thee that Thou hast heard Me. And I knew that Thou hearest Me always: but because of the people which stand by I said it, that they may believe that Thou hast sent Me." Here the disciples and the people were to be given the most convincing evidence in regard to the relationship existing between Christ and God. They were to be shown that Christ's claim was not a deception.

"And when He thus had spoken, He cried with a loud voice, Lazarus, come forth." His voice, clear and penetrating, pierces the ear of the dead. As He speaks, divinity flashes through humanity. In His face, which is lighted up by the glory of God, the people see the assurance of His power. Every eye is fastened on the entrance to the cave. Every ear is bent to catch the slightest sound. With intense and painful interest all wait for the test of Christ's divinity, the evidence that is to substantiate His claim to be the Son of God, or to extinguish the hope forever.

There is a stir in the silent tomb, and he who was dead stands at the door of the sepulcher. His movements are impeded by the graveclothes in which he was laid away, and Christ says to the astonished spectators, "Loose him, and let him go." Again they are shown that the human worker is to co-operate with God. Humanity is to work for humanity. Lazarus is set free, and stands before the company, not as one emaciated from disease, and with feeble, tottering limbs, but as a man in the prime of life, and in the vigor of a noble manhood. His eyes beam with intelligence and with love for his Saviour. He casts himself in adoration at the feet of Jesus.

The beholders are at first speechless with amazement. Then there follows an inexpressible scene of rejoicing and thanksgiving. The sisters receive their brother back to life as the gift of God, and with joyful tears they brokenly express their thanks to the Saviour. But while brother, sisters, and friends are rejoicing in this reunion, Jesus withdraws from the scene. When they look for the Life-giver, He is not to be found.

6

Priestly Plottings

This chapter is based on John 11:47-54.

Bethany was so near Jerusalem that the news of the raising of Lazarus was soon carried to the city. Through spies who had witnessed the miracle the Jewish rulers were speedily in possession of the facts. A meeting of the Sanhedrin was at once called to decide as to what should be done. Christ had now fully made manifest His control of death and the grave. That mighty miracle was the crowning evidence offered by God to men that He had sent His Son into the world for their salvation. It was a demonstration of divine power sufficient to convince every mind that was under the control of reason and enlightened conscience. Many who witnessed the resurrection of Lazarus were led to believe on Jesus. But the hatred of the priests against Him was intensified. They had rejected all lesser evidence of His divinity, and they were only enraged at this new miracle. The dead had been raised in the full light of day, and before a crowd of witnesses. No artifice could explain away such evidence. For this very reason the enmity of the priests grew deadlier. They were more than ever determined to put a stop to Christ's work.

The Sadducees, though not favorable to Christ, had not been so full of malignity toward Him as were the Pharisees. Their hatred had not been so bitter. But they were now thoroughly alarmed. They did not believe in a resurrection of the dead. Producing so-called science, they had reasoned that it would be an impossibility for a dead body to be brought to life. But by a few words from Christ their theory had been overthrown. They were shown to be ignorant both of the Scriptures and of the power of God. They could see no possibility of removing the impression made on the people by the miracle. How could men be turned away from Him who had prevailed to rob the grave of its dead? Lying reports were put in circulation, but the miracle could not be denied, and how to counteract its effect they knew not. Thus far the Sadducees had not encouraged the plan of putting Christ to death. But after the resurrection of Lazarus they decided that only by His death could His fearless denunciations against them be stopped.

The Pharisees believed in the resurrection, and they could not but see that this miracle was an evidence that the Messiah was among them. But they had ever opposed Christ's work. From the first they had hated Him because He had exposed their hypocritical pretensions. He had torn aside the cloak of rigorous rites under which their moral deformity was hidden. The pure religion that He taught had condemned their hollow professions of piety. They thirsted to be revenged upon Him for His pointed rebukes. They had tried to provoke Him to say or do something that would give them occasion to condemn Him. Several times they had attempted to stone Him, but He had quietly withdrawn, and they had lost sight of Him.

The miracles He performed on the Sabbath were all for the relief of the afflicted, but the Pharisees had sought to condemn Him as a Sabbathbreaker. They had tried to arouse the Herodians against Him. They represented that He was seeking to set up a rival kingdom, and consulted with them how to destroy Him. To excite the Romans against Him, they had represented Him as trying to subvert their authority. They had tried every pretext to cut Him off from influencing the people. But so far their attempts had been foiled. The multitudes who witnessed His works of mercy and heard His pure and holy teachings knew that these were not the deeds and words of a Sabbathbreaker or blasphemer. Even the officers sent by the Pharisees had been so influenced by His words that they could not lay hands on Him. In desperation the Jews had finally passed an edict that any man who professed faith in Jesus should be cast out of the synagogue.

So, as the priests, the rulers, and the elders gathered for consultation, it was their fixed determination to silence Him who did such marvelous works that all men wondered. Pharisees and Sadducees were more nearly united than ever before. Divided hitherto, they became one in their opposition to Christ. Nicodemus and Joseph had, in former councils, prevented the condemnation of Jesus, and for this reason they were not now summoned. There were present at the council other influential men who believed on Jesus, but their influence prevailed nothing against that of the malignant Pharisees.

Yet the members of the council were not all agreed. The Sanhedrin was not at this time a legal assembly. It existed only by tolerance. Some of its number questioned the wisdom of putting Christ to death. They feared that this would excite an insurrection among the people, causing the Romans to withhold further favors from the priesthood, and to take from them the power they still held. The Sadducees were united in their hatred of Christ, yet they were inclined to be cautious in their movements, fearing that the Romans would deprive them of their high standing.

In this council, assembled to plan the death of Christ, the Witness was present who heard the boastful words of Nebuchadnezzar, who witnessed the idolatrous feast of Belshazzar, who was present when Christ in Nazareth announced Himself the Anointed One. This Witness was now impressing the rulers with the work they were doing. Events in the life of Christ rose up before them with a distinctness that alarmed them. They remembered the scene in the temple, when Jesus, then a child of twelve, stood before the learned doctors of the law, asking them questions at which they wondered. The miracle just performed bore witness that Jesus was none other than the Son of God. In their true significance, the Old Testament Scriptures regarding Christ flashed before their minds. Perplexed and troubled, the rulers asked, "What do we?" There was a division in the council. Under the impression of the Holy Spirit, the priests and rulers could not banish the conviction that they were fighting against God.

While the council was at the height of its perplexity, Caiaphas the high priest arose. Caiaphas was a proud and cruel man, overbearing and intolerant. Among his family connections were Sadducees, proud, bold, reckless, full of ambition and cruelty, which they hid under a cloak of pretended righteousness. Caiaphas had studied the prophecies, and although ignorant of their true meaning, he spoke with great authority and assurance: "Ye know nothing at all, nor consider that it is expedient for us, that one man should die for the people, and that the whole nation perish not." Even if Jesus were innocent, urged the high priest, He must be put out of the way. He was troublesome, drawing the people to Himself, and lessening the authority of the rulers. He was only one; it was better that He should die than that the authority of the rulers should be weakened. If the people were to lose confidence in their rulers, the national power would be destroyed. Caiaphas urged that after this miracle the followers of Jesus would likely rise in revolt. The Romans will then come, he said, and will close our temple, and abolish our laws, destroying us as a nation. What is the life of this Galilean worth in comparison with the life of the nation? If He stands in the way of Israel's well-being, is it not doing God a service to remove Him? Better that one man perish than that the whole nation be destroyed.

In declaring that one man should die for the nation, Caiaphas indicated that he had some knowledge of the prophecies, although it was very limited. But John, in his account of this scene, takes up the prophecy, and shows its broad and deep significance. He says, "And not for that nation only, but that also He should gather together in one the children of God that were scattered abroad." How blindly did the haughty Caiaphas acknowledge the Saviour's mission!

On the lips of Caiaphas this most precious truth was turned into a lie. The policy he advocated was based on a principle borrowed from heathenism. Among the heathen, the dim consciousness that one was to die for the human race had led to the offering of human sacrifices. So Caiaphas proposed by the sacrifice of Jesus to save the guilty nation, not from transgression, but in transgression, that they might continue in sin. And by his reasoning he thought to silence the remonstrances of those who might dare to say that as yet nothing worthy of death had been found in Jesus.

At this council Christ's enemies had been deeply convicted. The Holy Spirit had impressed their minds. But Satan strove to gain control of them. He urged upon their notice the grievances they had suffered on account of Christ. How little He had honored their righteousness. He presented a righteousness far greater, which all who would be children of God must possess. Taking no notice of their forms and ceremonies, He had encouraged sinners to go directly to God as a merciful Father, and make known their wants. Thus, in their opinion, He had set aside the priesthood. He had refused to acknowledge the theology of the rabbinical schools. He had exposed the evil practices of the priests, and had irreparably hurt their influence. He had injured the effect of their maxims and traditions, declaring that though they strictly enforced the ritual law, they made void the law of God. All this Satan now brought to their minds.

Satan told them that in order to maintain their authority, they must put Jesus to death. This counsel they followed. The fact that they might lose the power they then exercised, was, they thought, sufficient reason for coming to some decision. With the exception of a few who dared not speak their minds, the Sanhedrin received the words of Caiaphas as the words of God. Relief came to the council; the discord ceased. They resolved to put Christ to death at the first favorable opportunity. In rejecting the proof of the divinity of Jesus, these priests and rulers had locked themselves in impenetrable darkness. They had come wholly under the sway of Satan, to be hurried by him over the brink of eternal ruin. Yet such was their deception that they were well pleased with themselves. They regarded themselves as patriots, who were seeking the nation's salvation.

The Sanhedrin feared, however, to take rash measures against Jesus, lest the people should become incensed, and the violence meditated toward Him should fall upon themselves. On this account the council delayed to execute the sentence they had pronounced. The Saviour understood the plotting of the priests. He knew that they longed to remove Him, and that their purpose would soon be accomplished. But it was not His place to hasten the crisis, and He withdrew from that region, taking the disciples with Him. Thus by His own example Jesus again enforced the instruction He had given to the disciples, "When they persecute you in this city, flee ye into another." Matt. 10:23. There was a wide field in which to work for the salvation of souls; and unless loyalty to Him required it, the Lord's servants were not to imperil their lives.

Jesus had now given three years of public labor to the world. His example of self-denial and disinterested benevolence was before them.

His life of purity, of suffering and devotion, was known to all. Yet this short period of three years was as long as the world could endure the presence of its Redeemer.

His life had been one of persecution and insult. Driven from Bethlehem by a jealous king, rejected by His own people at Nazareth, condemned to death without a cause at Jerusalem, Jesus, with His few faithful followers, found a temporary asylum in a strange city. He who was ever touched by human woe, who healed the sick, restored sight to the blind, hearing to the deaf, and speech to the dumb, who fed the hungry and comforted the sorrowful, was driven from the people He had labored to save. He who walked upon the heaving billows, and by a word silenced their angry roaring, who cast out devils that in departing acknowledged Him to be the Son of God, who broke the slumbers of the dead, who held thousands entranced by His words of wisdom, was unable to reach the hearts of those who were blinded by prejudice and hatred, and who stubbornly rejected the light.

7

The Law of
the New Kingdom

This chapter is based on Matthew 20:20-28; Mark 10:32-45; Luke 18:31-34.

The time of the Passover was drawing near, and again Jesus turned toward Jerusalem. In His heart was the peace of perfect oneness with the Father's will, and with eager steps He pressed on toward the place of sacrifice. But a sense of mystery, of doubt and fear, fell upon the disciples. The Saviour "went before them: and they were amazed; and as they followed, they were afraid."

Again Christ called the twelve about Him, and with greater definiteness than ever before, He opened to them His betrayal and sufferings. "Behold," He said, "we go up to Jerusalem, and all things that are written by the prophets concerning the Son of man shall be accomplished. For He shall be delivered unto the Gentiles, and shall be mocked, and spitefully entreated, and spitted on: and they shall scourge Him, and put Him to death: and the third day He shall rise again. And they understood none of these things: and this saying was hid from them, neither knew they the things which were spoken."

Had they not just before proclaimed everywhere, "The kingdom of heaven is at hand"? Had not Christ Himself promised that many should sit down with Abraham and Isaac and Jacob in the kingdom of God? Had He not promised to all who had left aught for His sake a hundredfold in this life, and a part in His kingdom? And had He not given to the twelve the special promise of positions of high honor in His kingdom,—to sit on thrones judging the twelve tribes of Israel? Even now He had said that all things written in the prophets concerning Him should be fulfilled. And had not the prophets foretold the glory of the Messiah's reign? In the light of these thoughts, His words in regard to betrayal, persecution, and death seemed vague and shadowy. Whatever difficulties might intervene, they believed that the kingdom was soon to be established.

John, the son of Zebedee, had been one of the first two disciples who had followed Jesus. He and his brother James had been among the first group who had left all for His service. Gladly they had forsaken home and friends that they might be with Him; they had walked and talked with Him; they had been with Him in the privacy of the home, and in the public assemblies. He had quieted their fears, delivered them from danger, relieved their sufferings, comforted their grief, and with patience and tenderness had taught them, till their hearts seemed linked with His, and in the ardor of their love they longed to be nearest to Him in His kingdom. At every possible opportunity, John took his place next the Saviour, and James longed to be honored with as close connection with Him.

Their mother was a follower of Christ, and had ministered to Him freely of her substance. With a mother's love and ambition for her sons, she coveted for them the most honored place in the new kingdom. For this she encouraged them to make request.

Together the mother and her sons came to Jesus, asking that He would grant a petition on which their hearts were set.

"What would ye that I should do for you?" He questioned.

The mother answered, "Grant that these my two sons may sit, the one on Thy right hand, and the other on the left, in Thy kingdom."

Jesus bears tenderly with them, not rebuking their selfishness in seeking preference above their brethren. He reads their hearts, He knows the depth of their attachment to Him. Their love is not a mere human affection; though defiled by the earthliness of its human channel, it is an outflowing from the fountain of His own redeeming love. He will not rebuke, but deepen and purify. He said, "Are ye able to drink of the cup that I shall drink of, and to be baptized with the baptism that I am baptized with?" They recall His mysterious words, pointing to trial and suffering, yet answer confidently, "We are able." They would count it highest honor to prove their loyalty by sharing all that is to befall their Lord.

"Ye shall drink indeed of My cup, and be baptized with the baptism that I am baptized with," He said; before Him a cross instead of a throne, two malefactors His companions at His right hand and His left. John and James were to share with their Master in suffering; the one, first of the brethren to perish with the sword; the other, longest of all to endure toil, and reproach, and persecution.

"But to sit on My right hand, and on My left," He continued, "is not Mine to give, but it shall be given to them for whom it is prepared of My Father." In the kingdom of God, position is not gained through favoritism. It is not earned, nor is it received through an arbitrary bestowal. It is the result of character. The crown and the throne are the tokens of a condition attained; they are the tokens of self-conquest through our Lord Jesus Christ.

Long afterward, when the disciple had been brought into sympathy with Christ through the fellowship of His sufferings, the Lord revealed to John what is the condition of nearness in His kingdom. "To him that overcometh," Christ said, "will I grant to sit with Me in My throne, even as I also overcame, and am set down with My Father in His throne." "Him that overcometh will I make a pillar in the temple of My God, and he shall go no more out: and I will write upon him the name of My God, … and I will write upon him My new name." Rev. 3:21, 12. So Paul the apostle wrote, "I am now ready to be offered, and the time of my departure is at hand. I have fought a good fight, I have finished my course, I have kept the faith: henceforth there is laid up for me a crown of righteousness, which the Lord, the righteous Judge, shall give me at that day." 2 Tim. 4:6-8.

The one who stands nearest to Christ will be he who on earth has drunk most deeply of the spirit of His self-sacrificing love,—love that "vaunteth not itself, is not puffed up, … seeketh not her own, is not easily provoked, thinketh no evil" (1 Cor. 13:4, 5),—love that moves the disciple, as it moved our Lord, to give all, to live and labor and sacrifice, even unto death, for the saving of humanity. This spirit was made manifest in the life of Paul. He said, "For to me to live is Christ;" for his life revealed Christ to men; "and to die is gain,"—gain to Christ; death itself would make manifest the power of His grace, and gather souls to Him. "Christ shall be magnified in my body," he said, "whether it be by life or by death." Phil. 1:21, 20.

When the ten heard of the request of James and John, they were much displeased. The highest place in the kingdom was just what every one of them was seeking for himself, and they were angry that the two disciples had gained a seeming advantage over them.

Again the strife as to which should be greatest seemed about to be renewed, when Jesus, calling them to Him, said to the indignant disciples, "Ye know that they which are accounted to rule over the Gentiles exercise lordship over them; and their great ones exercise authority upon them. But so shall it not be among you."

In the kingdoms of the world, position meant self-aggrandizement. The people were supposed to exist for the benefit of the ruling classes. Influence, wealth, education, were so many means of gaining control of the masses for the use of the leaders. The higher classes were to think, decide, enjoy, and rule; the lower were to obey and serve. Religion, like all things else, was a matter of authority. The people were expected to believe and practice as their superiors directed. The right of man as man, to think and act for himself, was wholly unrecognized.

Christ was establishing a kingdom on different principles. He called men, not to authority, but to service, the strong to bear the infirmities of the weak. Power, position, talent, education, placed their possessor under the greater obligation to serve his fellows. To even the lowliest of Christ's disciples it is said, "All things are for your sakes." 2 Cor. 4:15.

"The Son of man came not to be ministered unto, but to minister, and to give His life a ransom for many." Among His disciples Christ was in every sense a caretaker, a burden bearer. He shared their poverty, He practiced self-denial on their account, He went before them to smooth the more difficult places, and soon He would consummate His work on earth by laying down His life. The principle on which Christ acted is to actuate the members of the church which is His body. The plan and ground of salvation is love. In the kingdom of Christ those are greatest who follow the example He has given, and act as shepherds of His flock.

The words of Paul reveal the true dignity and honor of the Christian life: "Though I be free from all men, yet have I made myself servant unto all," "not seeking mine own profit, but the profit of many, that they may be saved." 1 Cor. 9:19; 10:33.

In matters of conscience the soul must be left untrammeled. No one is to control another's mind, to judge for another, or to prescribe his duty. God gives to every soul freedom to think, and to follow his own convictions. "Every one of us shall give account of himself to God." No one has a right to merge his own individuality in that of another. In all matters where principle is involved, "let every man be fully persuaded in his own mind." Rom. 14:12, 5. In Christ's kingdom there is no lordly oppression, no compulsion of manner. The angels of heaven do not come to the earth to rule, and to exact homage, but as messengers of mercy, to co-operate with men in uplifting humanity.

The principles and the very words of the Saviour's teaching, in their divine beauty, dwelt in the memory of the beloved disciple. To his latest days the burden of John's testimony to the churches was, "This is the message that ye heard from the beginning, that we should love one another." "Hereby perceive we the love of God, because He laid down His life for us: and we ought to lay down our lives for the brethren." 1 John 3:11, 16.

This was the spirit that pervaded the early church. After the outpouring of the Holy Spirit, "the multitude of them that believed were of one heart and of one soul: neither said any of them that aught of the things which he possessed was his own." "Neither was there any among them that lacked." "And with great power gave the apostles witness of the resurrection of the Lord Jesus: and great grace was upon them all." Acts 4:32, 34, 33.

8

Zacchaeus

This chapter is based on Luke 19:1-10.

On the way to Jerusalem "Jesus entered and passed through Jericho." A few miles from the Jordan, on the western edge of the valley that here spread out into a plain, the city lay in the midst of tropic verdure and luxuriance of beauty. With its palm trees and rich gardens watered by living springs, it gleamed like an emerald in the setting of limestone hills and desolate ravines that interposed between Jerusalem and the city of the plain.

Many caravans on their way to the feast passed through Jericho. Their arrival was always a festive season, but now a deeper interest stirred the people. It was known that the Galilean Rabbi who had so lately brought Lazarus to life was in the throng; and though whispers were rife as to the plottings of the priests, the multitudes were eager to do Him homage.

Jericho was one of the cities anciently set apart for the priests, and at this time large numbers of priests had their residence there. But the city had also a population of a widely different character. It was a great center of traffic, and Roman officials and soldiers, with strangers from different quarters, were found there, while the collection of customs made it the home of many publicans.

"The chief among the publicans," Zacchaeus, was a Jew, and detested by his countrymen. His rank and wealth were the reward of a calling they abhorred, and which was regarded as another name for injustice and extortion. Yet the wealthy customs officer was not altogether the hardened man of the world that he seemed. Beneath the appearance of worldliness and pride was a heart susceptible to divine influences. Zacchaeus had heard of Jesus. The report of One who had borne Himself with kindness and courtesy toward the proscribed classes had spread far and wide. In this chief of the publicans was awakened a longing for a better life. Only a few miles from Jericho, John the Baptist had preached at the Jordan, and Zacchaeus had heard of the call to repentance. The instruction to the publicans, "Exact no more than that which is appointed you" (Luke 3:13), though outwardly disregarded, had impressed his mind. He knew the Scriptures, and was convicted that his practice was wrong. Now, hearing the words reported to have come from the Great Teacher, he felt that he was a sinner in the sight of God. Yet what he had heard of Jesus kindled hope in his heart.

Repentance, reformation of life, was possible, even to him; was not one of the new Teacher's most trusted disciples a publican? Zacchaeus began at once to follow the conviction that had taken hold upon him, and to make restitution to those whom he had wronged.

Already he had begun thus to retrace his steps, when the news sounded through Jericho that Jesus was entering the town. Zacchaeus determined to see Him. He was beginning to realize how bitter are the fruits of sin, and how difficult the path of him who tries to return from a course of wrong. To be misunderstood, to be met with suspicion and distrust in the effort to correct his errors, was hard to bear. The chief publican longed to look upon the face of Him whose words had brought hope to his heart.

The streets were crowded, and Zacchaeus, who was small of stature, could see nothing over the heads of the people. None would give way for him; so, running a little in advance of the multitude, to where a wide-branching fig tree hung over the way, the rich tax collector climbed to a seat among the boughs, whence he could survey the procession as it passed below. The crowd comes near, it is going by, and Zacchaeus scans with eager eyes to discern the one figure he longs to see.

Above the clamor of priests and rabbis and the shouts of welcome from the multitude, that unuttered desire of the chief publican spoke to the heart of Jesus. Suddenly, just beneath the fig tree, a group halts, the company before and behind come to a standstill, and One looks upward whose glance seems to read the soul. Almost doubting his senses, the man in the tree hears the words, "Zacchaeus, make haste, and come down; for today I must abide at thy house."

The multitude give way, and Zacchaeus, walking as in a dream, leads the way toward his own home. But the rabbis look on with scowling faces, and murmur in discontent and scorn, "that He was gone to be guest with a man that is a sinner."

Zacchaeus had been overwhelmed, amazed, and silenced at the love and condescension of Christ in stooping to him, so unworthy. Now love and loyalty to his new-found Master unseal his lips. He will make public his confession and his repentance.

In the presence of the multitude, "Zacchaeus stood, and said unto the Lord; Behold, Lord, the half of my goods I give to the poor; and if I have taken anything from any man by false accusation, I restore him fourfold.

"And Jesus said unto him, This day is salvation come to this house, forsomuch as he also is a son of Abraham."

When the rich young ruler had turned away from Jesus, the disciples had marveled at their Master's saying, "How hard is it for them that trust in riches to enter into the kingdom of God!" They had exclaimed one to another, "Who then can be saved?" Now they had a demonstration of the truth of Christ's words, "The things which are impossible with men are possible with God." Mark 10:24, 26; Luke 18:27. They say how, through the grace of God, a rich man could enter into the kingdom.

Before Zacchaeus had looked upon the face of Christ, he had begun the work that made him manifest as a true penitent. Before being accused by man, he had confessed his sin. He had yielded to the conviction of the Holy Spirit, and had begun to carry out the teaching of the words written for ancient Israel as well as for ourselves. The Lord had said long before, "If thy brother be waxen poor, and fallen in decay with thee; then thou shalt relieve him: yea, though he be a stranger, or a sojourner; that he may live with thee. Take thou no usury of him, or increase: but fear thy God; that thy brother may live with thee. Thou shalt not give him thy money upon usury, nor lend him thy victuals for increase." "Ye shall not therefore oppress one another; but thou shalt fear thy God." Lev. 25:35-37, 17. These words had been spoken by Christ Himself when He was enshrouded in the pillar of cloud, and the very first response of Zacchaeus to the love of Christ was in manifesting compassion toward the poor and suffering.

Among the publicans there was a confederacy, so that they could oppress the people, and sustain one another in their fraudulent practices. In their extortion they were but carrying out what had become an almost universal custom. Even the priests and rabbis who despised them were guilty of enriching themselves by dishonest practices under cover of their sacred calling. But no sooner did Zacchaeus yield to the influence of the Holy Spirit than he cast aside every practice contrary to integrity.

No repentance is genuine that does not work reformation. The righteousness of Christ is not a cloak to cover unconfessed and unforsaken sin; it is a principle of life that transforms the character and controls the conduct. Holiness is wholeness for God; it is the entire surrender of heart and life to the indwelling of the principles of heaven.

The Christian in his business life is to represent to the world the manner in which our Lord would conduct business enterprises. In every transaction he is to make it manifest that God is his teacher. "Holiness unto the Lord" is to be written upon daybooks and ledgers, on deeds, receipts, and bills of exchange. Those who profess to be followers of Christ, and who deal in an unrighteous manner, are bearing false witness against the character of a holy, just, and merciful God. Every converted soul will, like Zacchaeus, signalize the entrance of Christ into his heart by an abandonment of the unrighteous practices that have marked his life. Like the chief publican, he will give proof of his sincerity by making restitution. The Lord says, "If the wicked restore the pledge, give again that he had robbed, walk in the statutes of life, without committing iniquity; ... none of his sins that he hath committed shall be mentioned unto him: ... He shall surely live." Ezek. 33:15, 16.

If we have injured others through any unjust business transaction, if we have overreached in trade, or defrauded any man, even though it be within the pale of the law, we should confess our wrong, and make restitution as far as lies in our power. It is right for us to restore not only that which we have taken, but all that it would have accumulated if put to a right and wise use during the time it has been in our possession.

To Zacchaeus the Saviour said, "This day is salvation come to this house." Not only was Zacchaeus himself blessed, but all his household with him. Christ went to his home to give him lessons of truth, and to instruct his household in the things of the kingdom. They had been shut out from the synagogues by the contempt of rabbis and worshipers; but now, the most favored household in all Jericho, they gathered in their own home about the divine Teacher, and heard for themselves the words of life.

It is when Christ is received as a personal Saviour that salvation comes to the soul. Zacchaeus had received Jesus, not merely as a passing guest in his home, but as One to abide in the soul temple. The scribes and Pharisees accused him as a sinner, they murmured against Christ for becoming his guest, but the Lord recognized him as a son of Abraham. For "they which are of faith, the same are the children of Abraham." Gal. 3:7.

9

The Feast at Simon's House

This chapter is based on Matt. 26:6-13; Mark 14:3-11; Luke 7:36-50; John 11:55-57; 12:1-11.

Simon of Bethany was accounted a disciple of Jesus. He was one of the few Pharisees who had openly joined Christ's followers. He acknowledged Jesus as a teacher, and hoped that He might be the Messiah, but he had not accepted Him as a Saviour. His character was not transformed; his principles were unchanged.

Simon had been healed of the leprosy, and it was this that had drawn him to Jesus. He desired to show his gratitude, and at Christ's last visit to Bethany he made a feast for the Saviour and His disciples. This feast brought together many of the Jews. There was at this time much excitement at Jerusalem. Christ and His mission were attracting greater attention than ever before. Those who had come to the feast closely watched His movements, and some of them with unfriendly eyes.

The Saviour had reached Bethany only six days before the Passover, and according to His custom had sought rest at the home of Lazarus. The crowds of travelers who passed on to the city spread the tidings that He was on His way to Jerusalem, and that He would rest over the Sabbath at Bethany. Among the people there was great enthusiasm. Many flocked to Bethany, some out of sympathy with Jesus, and others from curiosity to see one who had been raised from the dead.

Many expected to hear from Lazarus a wonderful account of scenes witnessed after death. They were surprised that he told them nothing. He had nothing of this kind to tell. Inspiration declares, "The dead know not anything. ... Their love, and their hatred, and their envy, is now perished." Eccl. 9:5, 6. But Lazarus did have a wonderful testimony to bear in regard to the work of Christ. He had been raised from the dead for this purpose. With assurance and power he declared that Jesus was the Son of God.

The reports carried back to Jerusalem by the visitors to Bethany increased the excitement. The people were eager to see and hear Jesus. There was a general inquiry as to whether Lazarus would accompany Him to Jerusalem, and if the prophet would be crowned king at the Passover. The priests and rulers saw that their hold upon the people was still weakening, and their rage against Jesus grew more bitter. They could hardly wait for the opportunity of removing Him forever from their way. As time passed, they began to fear that after all He might not come to Jerusalem.

They remembered how often He had baffled their murderous designs, and they were fearful that He had now read their purposes against Him, and would remain away. They could ill conceal their anxiety, and questioned among themselves, "What think ye, that He will not come to the feast?"

A council of the priests and Pharisees was called. Since the raising of Lazarus the sympathies of the people were so fully with Christ that it would be dangerous to seize upon Him openly. So the authorities determined to take Him secretly, and carry on the trial as quietly as possible. They hoped that when His condemnation became known, the fickle tide of public opinion would set in their favor.

Thus they proposed to destroy Jesus. But so long as Lazarus lived, the priests and rabbis knew that they were not secure. The very existence of a man who had been four days in the grave, and who had been restored by a word from Jesus, would sooner or later cause a reaction. The people would be avenged on their leaders for taking the life of One who could perform such a miracle. The Sanhedrin therefore decided that Lazarus also must die. To such lengths do envy and prejudice lead their slaves. The hatred and unbelief of the Jewish leaders had increased until they would even take the life of one whom infinite power had rescued from the grave.

While this plotting was going on at Jerusalem, Jesus and His friends were invited to Simon's feast. At the table the Saviour sat with Simon, whom He had cured of a loathsome disease, on one side, and Lazarus, whom He had raised from the dead, on the other. Martha served at the table, but Mary was earnestly listening to every word from the lips of Jesus. In His mercy, Jesus had pardoned her sins, He had called forth her beloved brother from the grave, and Mary's heart was filled with gratitude. She had heard Jesus speak of His approaching death, and in her deep love and sorrow she had longed to show Him honor. At great personal sacrifice she had purchased an alabaster box of "ointment of spikenard, very costly," with which to anoint His body. But now many were declaring that He was about to be crowned king. Her grief was turned to joy, and she was eager to be first in honoring her Lord. Breaking her box of ointment, she poured its contents upon the head and feet of Jesus; then, as she knelt weeping, moistening them with her tears, she wiped His feet with her long, flowing hair.

She had sought to avoid observation, and her movements might have passed unnoticed, but the ointment filled the room with its fragrance, and published her act to all present. Judas looked upon this act with great displeasure. Instead of waiting to hear what Christ would say of the matter, he began to whisper his complaints to those near him, throwing reproach upon Christ for suffering such waste. Craftily he made suggestions that would be likely to cause disaffection.

Judas was treasurer for the disciples, and from their little store he had secretly drawn for his own use, thus narrowing down their resources to a meager pittance. He was eager to put into the bag all that he could obtain. The treasure in the bag was often drawn upon to relieve the poor; and when something that Judas did not think essential was bought, he would say, Why is this waste? why was not the cost of this put into the bag that I carry for the poor? Now the act of Mary was in such marked contrast to his self-ishness that he was put to shame; and according to his custom, he sought to assign a worthy motive for his objection to her gift. Turning to the disciples, he asked, "Why was not this ointment sold for three hundred pence, and given to the poor? This he said, not that he cared for the poor; but because he was a thief, and had the bag, and bare what was put therein." Judas had no heart for the poor. Had Mary's ointment been sold, and the proceeds fallen into his possession, the poor would have received no benefit.

Judas had a high opinion of his own executive ability. As a financier he thought himself greatly superior to his fellow disciples, and he had led them to regard him in the same light. He had gained their confidence, and had a strong influence over them. His professed sympathy for the poor deceived them, and his artful insinuation caused them to look distrustfully upon Mary's devotion. The murmur passed round the table, "To what purpose is this waste? For this ointment might have been sold for much, and given to the poor."

Mary heard the words of criticism. Her heart trembled within her. She feared that her sister would reproach her for extravagance. The Master, too, might think her improvident. Without apology or excuse she was about to shrink away, when the voice of her Lord was heard, "Let her alone; why trouble ye her?" He saw that she was embarrassed and distressed. He knew that in this act of service she had expressed her gratitude for the forgive-ness of her sins, and He brought relief to her mind. Lifting His voice above the murmur of criticism, He said, "She hath wrought a good work on Me. For ye have the poor with you always, and whensoever ye will ye may do them good: but Me ye have not always. She hath done what she could: she is come aforehand to anoint My body to the burying."

The fragrant gift which Mary had thought to lavish upon the dead body of the Saviour she poured upon His living form. At the burial its sweet-ness could only have pervaded the tomb; now it gladdened His heart with the assurance of her faith and love. Joseph of Arimathaea and Nicodemus offered not their gift of love to Jesus in His life. With bitter tears they brought their costly spices for His cold, unconscious form. The women who bore spices to the tomb found their errand in vain, for He had risen. But Mary, pouring out her love upon the Saviour while He was conscious of her devotion, was anointing Him for the burial. And as He went down into the darkness of His great trial, He carried with Him the memory of that deed, an earnest of the love that would be His from His redeemed ones forever.

Many there are who bring their precious gifts for the dead. As they stand about the cold, silent form, words of love are freely spoken. Tenderness, appreciation, devotion, all are lavished upon one who sees not nor hears. Had these words been spoken when the weary spirit needed them so much, when the ear could hear and the heart could feel, how precious would have been their fragrance!

Mary knew not the full significance of her deed of love. She could not answer her accusers. She could not explain why she had chosen that occasion for anointing Jesus. The Holy Spirit had planned for her, and she had obeyed His promptings. Inspiration stoops to give no reason. An unseen presence, it speaks to mind and soul, and moves the heart to action. It is its own justification.

Christ told Mary the meaning of her act, and in this He gave her more than He had received. "In that she hath poured this ointment on My body," He said, "she did it for My burial." As the alabaster box was broken, and filled the whole house with its fragrance, so Christ was to die, His body was to be broken; but He was to rise from the tomb, and the fragrance of His life was to fill the earth. Christ "hath loved us, and hath given Himself for us an offering and a sacrifice to God for a sweet-smelling savor." Eph. 5:2.

"Verily I say unto you," Christ declared, "Wheresoever this gospel shall be preached throughout the whole world, this also that she hath done shall be spoken of for a memorial of her." Looking into the future, the Saviour spoke with certainty concerning His gospel. It was to be preached throughout the world. And as far as the gospel extended, Mary's gift would shed its fragrance, and hearts would be blessed through her unstudied act. Kingdoms would rise and fall; the names of monarchs and conquerors would be forgotten; but this woman's deed would be immortalized upon the pages of sacred history. Until time should be no more, that broken alabaster box would tell the story of the abundant love of God for a fallen race.

Mary's act was in marked contrast with that which Judas was about to do. What a sharp lesson Christ might have given him who had dropped the seed of criticism and evil thinking into the minds of the disciples! How justly the accuser might have been accused! He who reads the motives of every heart, and understands every action, might have opened before those at the feast dark chapters in the experience of Judas. The hollow pretense on which the traitor based his words might have been laid bare; for, instead of sympathizing with the poor, he was robbing them of the money intended for their relief. Indignation might have been excited against him for his oppression of the widow, the orphan, and the hireling. But had Christ unmasked Judas, this would have been urged as a reason for the betrayal. And though charged with being a thief, Judas would have gained sympathy, even among the disciples. The Saviour reproached him not, and thus avoided giving him an excuse for his treachery.

But the look which Jesus cast upon Judas convinced him that the Saviour penetrated his hypocrisy, and read his base, contemptible character. And in commending Mary's action, which had been so severely condemned, Christ had rebuked Judas. Prior to this, the Saviour had never given him a direct rebuke. Now the reproof rankled in his heart. He determined to be revenged. From the supper he went directly to the palace of the high priest, where he found the council assembled, and he offered to betray Jesus into their hands.

The priests were greatly rejoiced. These leaders of Israel had been given the privilege of receiving Christ as their Saviour, without money and without price. But they refused the precious gift offered them in the most tender spirit of constraining love. They refused to accept that salvation which is of more value than gold, and bought their Lord for thirty pieces of silver.

Judas had indulged avarice until it overpowered every good trait of his character. He grudged the offering made to Jesus. His heart burned with envy that the Saviour should be the recipient of a gift suitable for the monarchs of the earth. For a sum far less than the box of ointment cost, he betrayed his Lord.

The disciples were not like Judas. They loved the Saviour. But they did not rightly appreciate His exalted character. Had they realized what He had done for them, they would have felt that nothing bestowed upon Him was wasted. The wise men from the East, who knew so little of Jesus, had shown a truer appreciation of the honor due Him. They brought precious gifts to the Saviour, and bowed in homage before Him when He was but a babe, and cradled in a manger.

Christ values acts of heartfelt courtesy. When anyone did Him a favor, with heavenly politeness He blessed the actor. He did not refuse the simplest flower plucked by the hand of a child, and offered to Him in love. He accepted the offerings of children, and blessed the givers, inscribing their names in the book of life. In the Scriptures, Mary's anointing of Jesus is mentioned as distinguishing her from the other Marys. Acts of love and reverence for Jesus are an evidence of faith in Him as the Son of God. And the Holy Spirit mentions, as evidences of woman's loyalty to Christ: "If she have washed the saints' feet, if she have relieved the afflicted, if she have diligently followed every good work." 1 Tim. 5:10.

Christ delighted in the earnest desire of Mary to do the will of her Lord. He accepted the wealth of pure affection which His disciples did not, would not, understand. The desire that Mary had to do this service for her Lord was of more value to Christ than all the precious ointment in the world, because it expressed her appreciation of the world's Redeemer. It was the love of Christ that constrained her. The matchless excellence of the character of Christ filled her soul. That ointment was a symbol of the heart of the giver. It was the outward demonstration of a love fed by heavenly streams until it overflowed.

The work of Mary was just the lesson the disciples needed to show them that the expression of their love for Him would be pleasing to Christ. He had been everything to them, and they did not realize that soon they would be deprived of His presence, that soon they could offer Him no token of their gratitude for His great love. The loneliness of Christ, separated from the heavenly courts, living the life of humanity, was never understood or appreciated by the disciples as it should have been. He was often grieved because His disciples did not give Him that which He should have received from them. He knew that if they were under the influence of the heavenly angels that accompanied Him, they too would think no offering of sufficient value to declare the heart's spiritual affection.

Their afterknowledge gave them a true sense of the many things they might have done for Jesus expressive of the love and gratitude of their hearts, while they were near Him. When Jesus was no longer with them, and they felt indeed as sheep without a shepherd, they began to see how they might have shown Him attentions that would have brought gladness to His heart. They no longer cast blame upon Mary, but upon themselves. Oh, if they could have taken back their censuring, their presenting the poor as more worthy of the gift than was Christ! They felt the reproof keenly as they took from the cross the bruised body of their Lord.

The same want is evident in our world today. But few appreciate all that Christ is to them. If they did, the great love of Mary would be expressed, the anointing would be freely bestowed. The expensive ointment would not be called a waste. Nothing would be thought too costly to give for Christ, no self-denial or self-sacrifice too great to be endured for His sake.

The words spoken in indignation, "To what purpose is this waste?" brought vividly before Christ the greatest sacrifice ever made,—the gift of Himself as the propitiation for a lost world. The Lord would be so bountiful to His human family that it could not be said of Him that He could do more. In the gift of Jesus, God gave all heaven. From a human point of view, such a sacrifice was a wanton waste. To human reasoning the whole plan of salvation is a waste of mercies and resources. Self-denial and wholehearted sacrifice meet us everywhere. Well may the heavenly host look with amazement upon the human family who refuse to be uplifted and enriched with the boundless love expressed in Christ. Well may they exclaim, Why this great waste?

But the atonement for a lost world was to be full, abundant, and complete. Christ's offering was exceedingly abundant to reach every soul that God had created. It could not be restricted so as not to exceed the number who would accept the great Gift. All men are not saved; yet the plan of redemption is not a waste because it does not accomplish all that its liberality has provided for. There must be enough and to spare.

Simon the host had been influenced by the criticism of Judas upon Mary's gift, and he was surprised at the conduct of Jesus. His Pharisaic pride was offended. He knew that many of his guests were looking upon Christ with distrust and displeasure. Simon said in his heart, "This Man, if He were a prophet, would have known who and what manner of woman this is that toucheth Him: for she is a sinner."

By curing Simon of leprosy, Christ had saved him from a living death. But now Simon questioned whether the Saviour were a prophet. Because Christ allowed this woman to approach Him, because He did not indignantly spurn her as one whose sins were too great to be forgiven, because He did not show that He realized she had fallen, Simon was tempted to think that He was not a prophet. Jesus knows nothing of this woman who is so free in her demonstrations, he thought, or He would not allow her to touch Him.

But it was Simon's ignorance of God and of Christ that led him to think as he did. He did not realize that God's Son must act in God's way, with compassion, tenderness, and mercy. Simon's way was to take no notice of Mary's penitent service. Her act of kissing Christ's feet and anointing them with ointment was exasperating to his hardheartedness. He thought that if Christ were a prophet, He would recognize sinners and rebuke them.

To this unspoken thought the Saviour answered: "Simon, I have somewhat to say unto thee. ... There was a certain creditor which had two debtors: the one owed five hundred pence, and the other fifty. And when they had nothing to pay, he frankly forgave them both. Tell Me therefore, which of them will love him most? Simon answered and said, I suppose that he, to whom he forgave most. And He said unto him, Thou hast rightly judged."

As did Nathan with David, Christ concealed His home thrust under the veil of a parable. He threw upon His host the burden of pronouncing sentence upon himself. Simon had led into sin the woman he now despised. She had been deeply wronged by him. By the two debtors of the parable, Simon and the woman were represented. Jesus did not design to teach that different degrees of obligation should be felt by the two persons, for each owed a debt of gratitude that never could be repaid. But Simon felt himself more righteous than Mary, and Jesus desired him to see how great his guilt really was. He would show him that his sin was greater than hers, as much greater as a debt of five hundred pence exceeds a debt of fifty pence.

Simon now began to see himself in a new light. He saw how Mary was regarded by One who was more than a prophet. He saw that with keen prophetic eye Christ read her heart of love and devotion. Shame seized upon him, and he realized that he was in the presence of One superior to himself.

"I entered into thine house," Christ continued, "thou gavest Me no water for My feet;" but with tears of repentance, prompted by love, Mary hath washed My feet, and wiped them with the hair of her head. "Thou gavest Me no kiss: but this woman," whom you despise, "since the time I came in hath not ceased to kiss My feet." Christ recounted the opportunities Simon had had to show his love for his Lord, and his appreciation of what had been done for him. Plainly, yet with delicate politeness, the Saviour assured His disciples that His heart is grieved when His children neglect to show their gratitude to Him by words and deeds of love.

The Heart Searcher read the motive that led to Mary's action, and He saw also the spirit that prompted Simon's words. "Seest thou this woman?" He said to him. She is a sinner. "I say unto thee, Her sins, which are many, are forgiven; for she loved much: but to whom little is forgiven, the same loveth little."

Simon's coldness and neglect toward the Saviour showed how little he appreciated the mercy he had received. He had thought he honored Jesus by inviting Him to his house. But he now saw himself as he really was. While he thought himself reading his Guest, his Guest had been reading him. He saw how true Christ's judgment of him was. His religion had been a robe of Pharisaism. He had despised the compassion of Jesus. He had not recognized Him as the representative of God. While Mary was a sinner pardoned, he was a sinner unpardoned. The rigid rule of justice he had desired to enforce against her condemned him.

Simon was touched by the kindness of Jesus in not openly rebuking him before the guests. He had not been treated as he desired Mary to be treated. He saw that Jesus did not wish to expose his guilt to others, but sought by a true statement of the case to convince his mind, and by pitying kindness to subdue his heart. Stern denunciation would have hardened Simon against repentance, but patient admonition convinced him of his error. He saw the magnitude of the debt which he owed his Lord. His pride was humbled, he repented, and the proud Pharisee became a lowly, self-sacrificing disciple.

Mary had been looked upon as a great sinner, but Christ knew the circumstances that had shaped her life. He might have extinguished every spark of hope in her soul, but He did not. It was He who had lifted her from despair and ruin. Seven times she had heard His rebuke of the demons that controlled her heart and mind. She had heard His strong cries to the Father in her behalf. She knew how offensive is sin to His unsullied purity, and in His strength she had overcome.

When to human eyes her case appeared hopeless, Christ saw in Mary capabilities for good. He saw the better traits of her character. The plan of redemption has invested humanity with great possibilities, and in Mary these possibilities were to be realized. Through His grace she became a partaker of the divine nature. The one who had fallen, and whose mind had been a habitation of demons, was brought very near to the Saviour in fellowship and ministry. It was Mary who sat at His feet and learned of Him. It was Mary who poured upon His head the precious anointing oil, and bathed His feet with her tears. Mary stood beside the cross, and followed Him to the sepulcher. Mary was first at the tomb after His resurrection. It was Mary who first proclaimed a risen Saviour.

Jesus knows the circumstances of every soul. You may say, I am sinful, very sinful. You may be; but the worse you are, the more you need Jesus. He turns no weeping, contrite one away. He does not tell to any all that He might reveal, but He bids every trembling soul take courage. Freely will He pardon all who come to Him for forgiveness and restoration.

Christ might commission the angels of heaven to pour out the vials of His wrath on our world, to destroy those who are filled with hatred of God. He might wipe this dark spot from His universe. But He does not do this. He is today standing at the altar of incense, presenting before God the prayers of those who desire His help.

The souls that turn to Him for refuge, Jesus lifts above the accusing and the strife of tongues. No man or evil angel can impeach these souls. Christ unites them to His own divine-human nature. They stand beside the great Sin Bearer, in the light proceeding from the throne of God. "Who shall lay anything to the charge of God's elect? It is God that justifieth. Who is he that condemneth? It is Christ that died, yea rather, that is risen again, who is even at the right hand of God, who also maketh intercession for us." Rom. 8:33, 34.

10

A Doomed People

This chapter is based on Mark 11:11-14, 20, 21; Matthew 21:17-19.

The triumphal ride of Christ into Jerusalem was the dim foreshadowing of His coming in the clouds of heaven with power and glory, amid the triumph of angels and the rejoicing of the saints. Then will be fulfilled the words of Christ to the priests and Pharisees: "Ye shall not see Me henceforth, till ye shall say, Blessed is He that cometh in the name of the Lord." Matt. 23:39. In prophetic vision Zechariah was shown that day of final triumph; and he beheld also the doom of those who at the first advent had rejected Christ: "They shall look upon Me whom they have pierced, and they shall mourn for Him, as one mourneth for his only son, and shall be in bitterness for Him, as one that is in bitterness for his first-born." Zech. 12:10. This scene Christ foresaw when He beheld the city and wept over it. In the temporal ruin of Jerusalem He saw the final destruction of that people who were guilty of the blood of the Son of God.

The disciples saw the hatred of the Jews to Christ, but they did not yet see to what it would lead. They did not yet understand the true condition of Israel, nor comprehend the retribution that was to fall upon Jerusalem. This Christ opened to them by a significant object lesson.

The last appeal to Jerusalem had been in vain. The priests and rulers had heard the prophetic voice of the past echoed by the multitude, in answer to the question, "Who is this?" but they did not accept it as the voice of Inspiration. In anger and amazement they tried to silence the people. There were Roman officers in the throng, and to them His enemies denounced Jesus as the leader of a rebellion. They represented that He was about to take possession of the temple, and reign as king in Jerusalem.

But the calm voice of Jesus hushed for a moment the clamorous throng as He again declared that He had not come to establish a temporal rule; He should soon ascend to His Father, and His accusers would see Him no more until He should come again in glory. Then, too late for their salvation, they would acknowledge Him. These words Jesus spoke with sadness and with singular power. The Roman officers were silenced and subdued. Their hearts, though strangers to divine influence, were moved as they had never been moved before. In the calm, solemn face of Jesus they read love, benevolence, and quiet dignity. They were stirred by a sympathy they could not understand. Instead of arresting Jesus, they were more inclined to pay Him homage. Turning upon the priests and rulers, they charged them with creating the disturbance. These leaders, chagrined and defeated, turned to the people with their complaints, and disputed angrily among themselves.

Meanwhile Jesus passed unnoticed to the temple. All was quiet there, for the scene upon Olivet had called away the people. For a short time Jesus remained at the temple, looking upon it with sorrowful eyes. Then He withdrew with His disciples, and returned to Bethany. When the people sought for Him to place Him on the throne, He was not to be found.

The entire night Jesus spent in prayer, and in the morning He came again to the temple. On the way He passed a fig orchard. He was hungry, "and seeing a fig tree afar off having leaves, He came, if haply He might find anything thereon: and when He came to it, He found nothing but leaves; for the time of figs was not yet."

It was not the season for ripe figs, except in certain localities; and on the highlands about Jerusalem it might truly be said, "The time of figs was not yet." But in the orchard to which Jesus came, one tree appeared to be in advance of all the others. It was already covered with leaves. It is the nature of the fig tree that before the leaves open, the growing fruit appears. Therefore this tree in full leaf gave promise of well-developed fruit. But its appearance was deceptive. Upon searching its branches, from the lowest bough to the topmost twig, Jesus found "nothing but leaves." It was a mass of pretentious foliage, nothing more.

Christ uttered against it a withering curse. "No man eat fruit of thee hereafter forever," He said. The next morning, as the Saviour and His disciples were again on their way to the city, the blasted branches and drooping leaves attracted their attention. "Master," said Peter, "behold, the fig tree which Thou cursedst is withered away."

Christ's act in cursing the fig tree had astonished the disciples. It seemed to them unlike His ways and works. Often they had heard Him declare that He came not to condemn the world, but that the world through Him might be saved. They remembered His words, "The Son of man is not come to destroy men's lives, but to save them." Luke 9:56. His wonderful works had been done to restore, never to destroy. The disciples had known Him only as the Restorer, the Healer. This act stood alone. What was its purpose? they questioned.

God "delighteth in mercy." "As I live, saith the Lord God, I have no pleasure in the death of the wicked." Micah 7:18; Ezek. 33:11. To Him the work of destruction and the denunciation of judgment is a "strange work." Isa. 28:21. But it is in mercy and love that He lifts the veil from the future, and reveals to men the results of a course of sin.

The cursing of the fig tree was an acted parable. That barren tree, flaunting its pretentious foliage in the very face of Christ, was a symbol of the Jewish nation. The Saviour desired to make plain to His disciples the cause and the certainty of Israel's doom. For this purpose He invested the tree with moral qualities, and made it the expositor of divine truth. The Jews stood forth distinct from all other nations, professing allegiance to God. They had been specially favored by Him, and they laid claim to righteousness above every other people. But they were corrupted by the love of the world and the greed of gain. They boasted of their knowledge, but they were ignorant of the requirements of God, and were full of hypocrisy. Like the barren tree, they spread their pretentious branches aloft, luxuriant in appearance, and beautiful to the eye, but they yielded "nothing but leaves." The Jewish religion, with its magnificent temple, its sacred altars, its mitered priests and impressive ceremonies, was indeed fair in outward appearance, but humility, love, and benevolence were lacking.

All the trees in the fig orchard were destitute of fruit; but the leafless trees raised no expectation, and caused no disappointment. By these trees the Gentiles were represented. They were as destitute as were the Jews of godliness; but they had not professed to serve God. They made no boastful pretensions to goodness. They were blind to the works and ways of God. With them the time of figs was not yet. They were still waiting for a day which would bring them light and hope. The Jews, who had received greater blessings from God, were held accountable for their abuse of these gifts. The privileges of which they boasted only increased their guilt.

Jesus had come to the fig tree hungry, to find food. So He had come to Israel, hungering to find in them the fruits of righteousness. He had lavished on them His gifts, that they might bear fruit for the blessing of the world. Every opportunity and privilege had been granted them, and in return He sought their sympathy and co-operation in His work of grace. He longed to see in them self-sacrifice and compassion, zeal for God, and a deep yearning of soul for the salvation of their fellow men. Had they kept the law of God, they would have done the same unselfish work that Christ did. But love to God and man was eclipsed by pride and self-sufficiency. They brought ruin upon themselves by refusing to minister to others. The treasures of truth which God had committed to them, they did not give to the world. In the barren tree they might read both their sin and its punishment. Withered beneath the Saviour's curse, standing forth sere and blasted, dried up by the roots, the fig tree showed what the Jewish people would be when the grace of God was removed from them. Refusing to impart blessing, they would no longer receive it. "O Israel," the Lord says, "thou hast destroyed thyself." Hosea 13:9.

The warning is for all time. Christ's act in cursing the tree which His own power had created stands as a warning to all churches and to all Christians. No one can live the law of God without ministering to others. But there are many who do not live out Christ's merciful, unselfish life. Some who think themselves excellent Christians do not understand what constitutes service for God. They plan and study to please themselves. They act only in reference to self. Time is of value to them only as they can gather for themselves. In all the affairs of life this is their object. Not for others but for themselves do they minister. God created them to live in a world where unselfish service must be performed. He designed them to help their fellow men in every possible way. But self is so large that they cannot see anything else. They are not in touch with humanity. Those who thus live for self are like the fig tree, which made every pretension but was fruitless. They observe the forms of worship, but without repentance or faith. In profession they honor the law of God, but obedience is lacking. They say, but do not. In the sentence pronounced on the fig tree Christ demonstrates how hateful in His eyes is this vain pretense. He declares that the open sinner is less guilty than is he who professes to serve God, but who bears no fruit to His glory.

The parable of the fig tree, spoken before Christ's visit to Jerusalem, had a direct connection with the lesson He taught in cursing the fruitless tree. For the barren tree of the parable the gardener pleaded, Let it alone this year, until I shall dig about it and dress it; and if it bear fruit, well; but if not, then after that thou shalt cut it down. Increased care was to be given the unfruitful tree. It was to have every advantage. But if it remained fruitless, nothing could save it from destruction. In the parable the result of the gardener's work was not foretold. It depended upon that people to whom Christ's words were spoken. They were represented by the fruitless tree, and it rested with them to decide their own destiny. Every advantage that Heaven could bestow was given them, but they did not profit by their increased blessings. By Christ's act in cursing the barren fig tree, the result was shown. They had determined their own destruction.

For more than a thousand years the Jewish nation had abused God's mercy and invited His judgments. They had rejected His warnings and slain His prophets. For these sins the people of Christ's day made themselves responsible by following the same course. In the rejection of their present mercies and warnings lay the guilt of that generation. The fetters which the nation had for centuries been forging, the people of Christ's day were fastening upon themselves.

In every age there is given to men their day of light and privilege, a probationary time in which they may become reconciled to God. But there is a limit to this grace. Mercy may plead for years and be slighted and rejected; but there comes a time when mercy makes her last plea. The heart becomes so hardened that it ceases to respond to the Spirit of God. Then the sweet, winning voice entreats the sinner no longer, and reproofs and warnings cease.

That day had come to Jerusalem. Jesus wept in anguish over the doomed city, but He could not deliver her. He had exhausted every resource. In rejecting the warnings of God's Spirit, Israel had rejected the only means of help. There was no other power by which they could be delivered.

The Jewish nation was a symbol of the people of all ages who scorn the pleadings of Infinite Love. The tears of Christ when He wept over Jerusalem were for the sins of all time. In the judgments pronounced upon Israel, those who reject the reproofs and warnings of God's Holy Spirit, may read their own condemnation.

In this generation there are many who are treading on the same ground as were the unbelieving Jews. They have witnessed the manifestation of the power of God; the Holy Spirit has spoken to their hearts; but they cling to their unbelief and resistance. God sends them warnings and reproof, but they are not willing to confess their errors, and they reject His message and His messenger. The very means He uses for their recovery becomes to them a stone of stumbling.

The prophets of God were hated by apostate Israel because through them their hidden sins were brought to light. Ahab regarded Elijah as his enemy because the prophet was faithful to rebuke the king's secret iniquities. So today the servant of Christ, the reprover of sin, meets with scorn and rebuffs. Bible truth, the religion of Christ, struggles against a strong current of moral impurity. Prejudice is even stronger in the hearts of men now than in Christ's day. Christ did not fulfill men's expectations; His life was a rebuke to their sins, and they rejected Him. So now the truth of God's word does not harmonize with men's practices and their natural inclination, and thousands reject its light. Men prompted by Satan cast doubt upon God's word, and choose to exercise their independent judgment. They choose darkness rather than light, but they do it at the peril of their souls. Those who caviled at the words of Christ, found ever-increased cause for cavil, until they turned from the Truth and the Life. So it is now. God does not propose to remove every objection which the carnal heart may bring against His truth. To those who refuse the precious rays of light which would illuminate the darkness, the mysteries of God's word remain such forever. From them the truth is hidden. They walk blindly, and know not the ruin before them.

Christ overlooked the world and all ages from the height of Olivet; and His words are applicable to every soul who slights the pleadings of divine mercy. Scorner of His love, He addresses you today. It is "thou, even thou," who shouldest know the things that belong to thy peace. Christ is shedding bitter tears for you, who have no tears to shed for yourself. Already that fatal hardness of heart which destroyed the Pharisees is manifest in you. And every evidence of the grace of God, every ray of divine light, is either melting and subduing the soul, or confirming it in hopeless impenitence.

Christ foresaw that Jerusalem would remain obdurate and impenitent; yet all the guilt, all the consequences of rejected mercy, lay at her own door. Thus it will be with every soul who is following the same course. The Lord declares, "O Israel, thou hast destroyed thyself." "Hear, O earth: behold, I will bring evil upon this people, even the fruit of their thoughts, because they have not hearkened unto My words, nor to My law, but rejected it." Hosea 13:9; Jer. 6:19.

11

The Temple Cleansed Again

This chapter is based on Matthew 21:12-16, 23-46;
Mark 11:15-19, 27-33; 12:1-12; Luke 19:45-48; 20:1-19.

At the beginning of His ministry, Christ had driven from the temple those who defiled it by their unholy traffic; and His stern and god-like demeanor had struck terror to the hearts of the scheming traders. At the close of His mission He came again to the temple, and found it still desecrated as before. The condition of things was even worse than before. The outer court of the temple was like a vast cattle yard. With the cries of the animals and the sharp chinking of coin was mingled the sound of angry altercation between traffickers, and among them were heard the voices of men in sacred office. The dignitaries of the temple were themselves engaged in buying and selling and the exchange of money. So completely were they controlled by their greed of gain that in the sight of God they were no better than thieves.

Little did the priests and rulers realize the solemnity of the work which it was theirs to perform. At every Passover and Feast of Tabernacles, thousands of animals were slain, and their blood was caught by the priests and poured upon the altar. The Jews had become familiar with the offering of blood, and had almost lost sight of the fact that it was sin which made necessary all this shedding of the blood of beasts. They did not discern that it prefigured the blood of God's dear Son, which was to be shed for the life of the world, and that by the offering of sacrifices men were to be directed to a crucified Redeemer.

Jesus looked upon the innocent victims of sacrifice, and saw how the Jews had made these great convocations scenes of bloodshed and cruelty. In place of humble repentance of sin, they had multiplied the sacrifice of beasts, as if God could be honored by a heartless service. The priests and rulers had hardened their hearts through selfishness and avarice. The very symbols pointing to the Lamb of God they had made a means of getting gain. Thus in the eyes of the people the sacredness of the sacrificial service had been in a great measure destroyed. The indignation of Jesus was stirred; He knew that His blood, so soon to be shed for the sins of the world, would be as little appreciated by the priests and elders as was the blood of beasts which they kept incessantly flowing.

Against these practices Christ had spoken through the prophets. Samuel had said, "Hath the Lord as great delight in burnt offerings and sacrifices, as in obeying the voice of the Lord? Behold, to obey is better than sacrifice, and to hearken than the fat of rams." And Isaiah, seeing in prophetic vision the apostasy of the Jews, addressed them as rulers of Sodom and Gomorrah: "Hear the word of the Lord, ye rulers of Sodom; give ear unto the law of our God, ye people of Gomorrah. To what purpose is the multitude of your sacrifices unto Me? saith the Lord: I am full of the burnt offerings of rams, and the fat of fed beasts; and I delight not in the blood of bullocks, or of lambs, or of he-goats. When ye come to appear before Me, who hath required this at your hand, to tread My courts?" "Wash you, make you clean; put away the evil of your doings from before Mine eyes; cease to do evil; learn to do well; seek judgment, relieve the oppressed, judge the fatherless, plead for the widow." 1 Sam. 15:22; Isa. 1:10-12, 16,17.

He who had Himself given these prophecies now for the last time repeated the warning. In fulfillment of prophecy the people had proclaimed Jesus king of Israel. He had received their homage, and accepted the office of king. In this character He must act. He knew that His efforts to reform a corrupt priesthood would be in vain; nevertheless His work must be done; to an unbelieving people the evidence of His divine mission must be given.

Again the piercing look of Jesus swept over the desecrated court of the temple. All eyes were turned toward Him. Priest and ruler, Pharisee and Gentile, looked with astonishment and awe upon Him who stood before them with the majesty of heaven's King. Divinity flashed through humanity, investing Christ with a dignity and glory He had never manifested before. Those standing nearest Him drew as far away as the crowd would permit. Except for a few of His disciples, the Saviour stood alone. Every sound was hushed. The deep silence seemed unbearable. Christ spoke with a power that swayed the people like a mighty tempest: "It is written, My house shall be called the house of prayer; but ye have made it a den of thieves." His voice sounded like a trumpet through the temple. The displeasure of His countenance seemed like consuming fire. With authority He commanded, "Take these things hence." John 2:16.

Three years before, the rulers of the temple had been ashamed of their flight before the command of Jesus. They had since wondered at their own fears, and their unquestioning obedience to a single humble Man. They had felt that it was impossible for their undignified surrender to be repeated. Yet they were now more terrified than before, and in greater haste to obey His command. There were none who dared question His authority. Priests and traders fled from His presence, driving their cattle before them.

On the way from the temple they were met by a throng who came with their sick inquiring for the Great Healer. The report given by the fleeing people caused some of these to turn back. They feared to meet One so powerful, whose very look had driven the priests and rulers from His presence. But a large number pressed through the hurrying crowd, eager to reach Him who was their only hope. When the multitude fled from the temple, many had remained behind. These were now joined by the newcomers. Again the temple court was filled by the sick and the dying, and once more Jesus ministered to them.

After a season the priests and rulers ventured back to the temple. When the panic had abated, they were seized with anxiety to know what would be the next movement of Jesus. They expected Him to take the throne of David. Quietly returning to the temple, they heard the voices of men, women, and children praising God. Upon entering, they stood transfixed before the wonderful scene. They saw the sick healed, the blind restored to sight, and deaf receive their hearing, and the crippled leap for joy. The children were foremost in the rejoicing. Jesus had healed their maladies; He had clasped them in His arms, received their kisses of grateful affection, and some of them had fallen asleep upon His breast as He was teaching the people. Now with glad voices the children sounded His praise. They repeated the hosannas of the day before, and waved palm branches triumphantly before the Saviour. The temple echoed and re-echoed with their acclamations, "Blessed be He that cometh in the name of the Lord!" "Behold, thy King cometh unto thee; He is just, and having salvation!" Ps. 118:26; Zech. 9:9. "Hosanna to the Son of David!"

The sound of these happy, unrestrained voices was an offense to the rulers of the temple. They set about putting a stop to such demonstrations. They represented to the people that the house of God was desecrated by the feet of the children and the shouts of rejoicing. Finding that their words made no impression on the people, the rulers appealed to Christ: "Hearest Thou what these say? And Jesus saith unto them, Yea; have ye never read, Out of the mouth of babes and sucklings Thou hast perfected praise?" Prophecy had foretold that Christ should be proclaimed as king, and that word must be fulfilled. The priests and rulers of Israel refused to herald His glory, and God moved upon the children to be His witnesses. Had the voices of the children been silent, the very pillars of the temple would have sounded the Saviour's praise.

The Pharisees were utterly perplexed and disconcerted. One whom they could not intimidate was in command. Jesus had taken His position as guardian of the temple. Never before had He assumed such kingly authority. Never before had His words and works possessed so great power. He had done marvelous works throughout Jerusalem, but never before in a manner so solemn and impressive. In presence of the people who had witnessed His wonderful works, the priests and rulers dared not show Him open hostility. Though enraged and confounded by His answer, they were unable to accomplish anything further that day.

The next morning the Sanhedrin again considered what course to pursue toward Jesus. Three years before, they had demanded a sign of His Messiahship. Since that time He had wrought mighty works throughout the land. He had healed the sick, miraculously fed thousands of people, walked upon the waves, and spoken peace to the troubled sea. He had repeatedly read the hearts of men as an open book; He had cast out demons, and raised the dead. The rulers had before them the evidences of His Messiahship. They now decided to demand no sign of His authority, but to draw out some admission or declaration by which He might be condemned.

Repairing to the temple where He was teaching, they proceeded to question Him: "By what authority doest Thou these things? and who gave Thee this authority?" They expected Him to claim that His authority was from God. Such an assertion they intended to deny. But Jesus met them with a question apparently pertaining to another subject, and He made His reply to them conditional on their answering this question. "The baptism of John," He said, "whence was it? from heaven, or of men?"

The priests saw that they were in a dilemma from which no sophistry could extricate them. If they said that John's baptism was from heaven, their inconsistency would be made apparent. Christ would say, Why have ye not then believed on him? John had testified of Christ, "Behold the Lamb of God, which taketh away the sin of the world." John 1:29. If the priests believed John's testimony, how could they deny the Messiahship of Christ? If they declared their real belief, that John's ministry was of men, they would bring upon themselves a storm of indignation; for the people believed John to be a prophet.

With intense interest the multitude awaited the decision. They knew that the priests had professed to accept the ministry of John, and they expected them to acknowledge without a question that he was sent from God. But after conferring secretly together, the priests decided not to commit themselves. Hypocritically professing ignorance, they said, "We cannot tell." "Neither tell I you," said Christ, "by what authority I do these things."

Scribes, priests, and rulers were all silenced. Baffled and disappointed, they stood with lowering brows, not daring to press further questions upon Christ. By their cowardice and indecision they had in a great measure forfeited the respect of the people, who now stood by, amused to see these proud, self-righteous men defeated.

All these sayings and doings of Christ were important, and their influence was to be felt in an ever-increasing degree after His crucifixion and ascension. Many of those who had anxiously awaited the result of the questioning of Jesus were finally to become His disciples, first drawn toward Him by His words on that eventful day. The scene in the temple court was never to fade from their minds. The contrast between Jesus and the high priest as they talked together was marked. The proud dignitary of the temple was clothed in rich and costly garments. Upon his head was a glittering tiara. His bearing was majestic, his hair and his long flowing beard were silvered by age. His appearance awed the beholders. Before this august personage stood the Majesty of heaven, without adornment or display. His garments were travel stained; His face was pale, and expressed a patient sadness; yet written there were dignity and benevolence that contrasted strangely with the proud, self-confident, and angry air of the high priest. Many of those who witnessed the words and deeds of Jesus in the temple from that time enshrined Him in their hearts as a prophet of God. But as the popular feeling turned in His favor, the hatred of the priests toward Jesus increased. The wisdom by which He escaped the snares set for His feet, being a new evidence of His divinity, added fuel to their wrath.

In His contest with the rabbis, it was not Christ's purpose to humiliate His opponents. He was not glad to see them in a hard place. He had an important lesson to teach. He had mortified His enemies by allowing them to be entangled in the net they had spread for Him. Their acknowledged ignorance in regard to the character of John's baptism gave Him an opportunity to speak, and He improved the opportunity by presenting before them their real position, adding another warning to the many already given.

"What think ye?" He said. "A certain man had two sons; and he came to the first, and said, Son, go work today in my vineyard. He answered and said, I will not: but afterward he repented, and went. And he came to the second, and said likewise. And he answered and said, I go, sir: and went not. Whether of them twain did the will of his father?"

This abrupt question threw His hearers off their guard. They had followed the parable closely, and now immediately answered, "The first." Fixing His steady eye upon them, Jesus responded in stern and solemn tones: "Verily I say unto you, That the publicans and the harlots go into the kingdom of God before you. For John came unto you in the way of righteousness, and ye believed him not: but the publicans and the harlots believed him: and ye, when ye had seen it, repented not afterward, that ye might believe him."

The priests and rulers could not but give a correct answer to Christ's question, and thus He obtained their opinion in favor of the first son. This son represented the publicans, those who were despised and hated by the Pharisees. The publicans had been grossly immoral. They had indeed been transgressors of the law of God, showing in their lives an absolute resistance to His requirements. They had been unthankful and unholy; when told to go and work in the Lord's vineyard, they had given a contemptuous refusal. But when John came, preaching repentance and baptism, the publicans received his message and were baptized.

The second son represented the leading men of the Jewish nation. Some of the Pharisees had repented and received the baptism of John; but the leaders would not acknowledge that he came from God. His warnings and denunciations did not lead them to reformation. They "rejected the counsel of God against themselves, being not baptized of him." Luke 7:30. They treated his message with disdain. Like the second son, who, when called, said, "I go, sir," but went not, the priests and rulers professed obedience, but acted disobedience. They made great professions of piety, they claimed to be obeying the law of God, but they rendered only a false obedience. The publicans were denounced and cursed by the Pharisees as infidels; but they showed by their faith and works that they were going into the kingdom of heaven before those self-righteous men who had been given great light, but whose works did not correspond to their profession of godliness.

The priests and rulers were unwilling to bear these searching truths; they remained silent, however, hoping that Jesus would say something which they could turn against Him; but they had still more to bear.

"Hear another parable," Christ said: "There was a certain householder, which planted a vineyard, and hedged it round about, and digged a wine press in it, and built a tower, and let it out to husbandmen, and went into a far country: and when the time of the fruit drew near, he sent his servants to the husbandmen, that they might receive the fruits of it. And the husbandmen took his servants, and beat one, and killed another, and stoned another. Again, he sent other servants more than the first: and they did unto them likewise. But last of all he sent unto them his son, saying, They will reverence my son. But when the husbandmen saw the son, they said among themselves, This is the heir; come, let us kill him, and let us seize on his inheritance. And they caught him, and cast him out of the vineyard, and slew him. When the lord therefore of the vineyard cometh, what will he do unto those husbandmen?"

Jesus addressed all the people present; but the priests and rulers answered. "He will miserably destroy those wicked men," they said, "and will let out his vineyard unto other husbandmen, which shall render him the fruits in their seasons." The speakers had not at first perceived the application of the parable, but they now saw that they had pronounced their own condemnation. In the parable the householder represented God, the vineyard the Jewish nation, and the hedge the divine law which was their protection. The tower was a symbol of the temple. The lord of the vineyard had done everything needful for its prosperity. "What could have been done more to my vineyard," he says, "that I have not done in it." Isa. 5:4. Thus was represented God's unwearied care for Israel. And as the husbandmen were to return to the lord a due proportion of the fruits of the vineyard, so God's people were to honor Him by a life corresponding to their sacred privileges. But as the husbandmen had killed the servants whom the master sent to them for fruit, so the Jews had put to death the prophets whom God sent to call them to repentance. Messenger after messenger had been slain. Thus far the application of the parable could not be questioned, and in what followed it was not less evident. In the beloved son whom the lord of the vineyard finally sent to his disobedient servants, and whom they seized and slew, the priests and rulers saw a distinct picture of Jesus and His impending fate. Already they were planning to slay Him whom the Father had sent to them as a last appeal. In the retribution inflicted upon the ungrateful husbandmen was portrayed the doom of those who should put Christ to death.

Looking with pity upon them, the Saviour continued, "Did ye never read in the Scriptures, The stone which the builders rejected, the same is become the head of the corner: this is the Lord's doing, and it is marvelous in our eyes? Therefore say I unto you, The kingdom of God shall be taken from you, and given to a nation bringing forth the fruits thereof. And whosoever shall fall on this stone shall be broken: but on whomsoever it shall fall, it will grind him to powder."

This prophecy the Jews had often repeated in the synagogues, applying it to the coming Messiah. Christ was the cornerstone of the Jewish economy, and of the whole plan of salvation. This foundation stone the Jewish builders, the priests and rulers of Israel, were now rejecting. The Saviour called their attention to the prophecies that would show them their danger. By every means in His power He sought to make plain to them the nature of the deed they were about to do.

And His words had another purpose. In asking the question, "When the lord therefore of the vineyard cometh, what will he do unto those husbandmen?" Christ designed that the Pharisees should answer as they did.

He designed that they should condemn themselves. His warnings, failing to arouse them to repentance, would seal their doom, and He wished them to see that they had brought ruin on themselves. He designed to show them the justice of God in the withdrawal of their national privileges, which had already begun, and which would end, not only in the destruction of their temple and their city, but in the dispersion of the nation.

The hearers recognized the warning. But notwithstanding the sentence they themselves had pronounced, the priests and rulers were ready to fill out the picture by saying, "This is the heir; come, let us kill him." "But when they sought to lay hands on Him, they feared the multitude," for the public sentiment was in Christ's favor.

In quoting the prophecy of the rejected stone, Christ referred to an actual occurrence in the history of Israel. The incident was connected with the building of the first temple. While it had a special application at the time of Christ's first advent, and should have appealed with special force to the Jews, it has also a lesson for us. When the temple of Solomon was erected, the immense stones for the walls and the foundation were entirely prepared at the quarry; after they were brought to the place of building, not an instrument was to be used upon them; the workmen had only to place them in position. For use in the foundation, one stone of unusual size and peculiar shape had been brought; but the workmen could find no place for it, and would not accept it. It was an annoyance to them as it lay unused in their way. Long it remained a rejected stone. But when the builders came to the laying of the corner, they searched for a long time to find a stone of sufficient size and strength, and of the proper shape, to take that particular place, and bear the great weight which would rest upon it. Should they make an unwise choice for this important place, the safety of the entire building would be endangered. They must find a stone capable of resisting the influence of the sun, of frost, and of tempest. Several stones had at different times been chosen, but under the pressure of immense weights they had crumbled to pieces. Others could not bear the test of the sudden atmospheric changes. But at last attention was called to the stone so long rejected. It had been exposed to the air, to sun and storm, without revealing the slightest crack. The builders examined this stone. It had borne every test but one. If it could bear the test of severe pressure, they decided to accept it for the cornerstone. The trial was made. The stone was accepted, brought to its assigned position, and found to be an exact fit. In prophetic vision, Isaiah was shown that this stone was a symbol of Christ. He says:

"Sanctify the Lord of hosts Himself; and let Him be your fear, and let Him be your dread. And He shall be for a sanctuary; but for a stone of stumbling and for a rock of offense to both the houses of Israel, for a gin and for a snare to the inhabitants of Jerusalem. And many among them shall stumble, and fall, and be broken, and be snared, and be taken." Carried down in prophetic vision to the first advent, the prophet is shown that Christ is to bear trials and tests of which the treatment of the chief cornerstone in the temple of Solomon was symbolic. "Therefore thus saith the Lord God, Behold, I lay in Zion for a foundation a stone, a tried stone, a precious cornerstone, a sure foundation: he that believeth shall not make haste." Isa. 8:13-15; 28:16.

In infinite wisdom, God chose the foundation stone, and laid it Himself. He called it "a sure foundation." The entire world may lay upon it their burdens and griefs; it can endure them all. With perfect safety they may build upon it. Christ is a "tried stone." Those who trust in Him, He never disappoints. He has borne every test. He has endured the pressure of Adam's guilt, and the guilt of his posterity, and has come off more than conqueror of the powers of evil. He has borne the burdens cast upon Him by every repenting sinner. In Christ the guilty heart has found relief. He is the sure foundation. All who make Him their dependence rest in perfect security.

In Isaiah's prophecy, Christ is declared to be both a sure foundation and a stone of stumbling. The apostle Peter, writing by inspiration of the Holy Spirit, clearly shows to whom Christ is a foundation stone, and to whom a rock of offense:

"If so be ye have tasted that the Lord is gracious. To whom coming, as unto a living stone, disallowed indeed of men, but chosen of God, and precious, ye also, as lively stones, are built up a spiritual house, an holy priesthood, to offer up spiritual sacrifices, acceptable to God by Jesus Christ. Wherefore also it is contained in the Scripture, Behold, I lay in Sion a chief cornerstone, elect, precious: and he that believeth on Him shall not be confounded. Unto you therefore which believe He is precious: but unto them which be disobedient, the stone which the builders disallowed, the same is made the head of the corner, and a stone of stumbling, and a rock of offense, even to them which stumble at the word, being disobedient." 1 Peter 2:3-8.

To those who believe, Christ is the sure foundation. These are they who fall upon the Rock and are broken. Submission to Christ and faith in Him are here represented. To fall upon the Rock and be broken is to give up our self-righteousness and to go to Christ with the humility of a child, repenting of our transgressions, and believing in His forgiving love. And so also it is by faith and obedience that we build on Christ as our foundation.

Upon this living stone, Jews and Gentiles alike may build. This is the only foundation upon which we may securely build. It is broad enough for all, and strong enough to sustain the weight and burden of the whole world. And by connection with Christ, the living stone, all who build upon this foundation become living stones. Many persons are by their own endeavors hewn, polished, and beautified; but they cannot become "living stones," because they are not connected with Christ. Without this connection, no man can be saved. Without the life of Christ in us, we cannot withstand the storms of temptation. Our eternal safety depends upon our building upon the sure foundation. Multitudes are today building upon foundations that have not been tested. When the rain falls, and the tempest rages, and the floods come, their house will fall, because it is not founded upon the eternal Rock, the chief cornerstone Christ Jesus.

"To them which stumble at the word, being disobedient," Christ is a rock of offense. But "the stone which the builders disallowed, the same is made the head of the corner." Like the rejected stone, Christ in His earthly mission had borne neglect and abuse. He was "despised and rejected of men; a man of sorrows, and acquainted with grief: ... He was despised, and we esteemed Him not." Isa. 53:3. But the time was near when He would be glorified. By the resurrection from the dead He would be declared "the Son of God with power." Rom. 1:4. At His second coming He would be revealed as Lord of heaven and earth. Those who were now about to crucify Him would recognize His greatness. Before the universe the rejected stone would become the head of the corner.

And on "whomsoever it shall fall, it will grind him to powder." The people who rejected Christ were soon to see their city and their nation destroyed. Their glory would be broken, and scattered as the dust before the wind. And what was it that destroyed the Jews? It was the rock which, had they built upon it, would have been their security. It was the goodness of God despised, the righteousness spurned, the mercy slighted. Men set themselves in opposition to God, and all that would have been their salvation was turned to their destruction. All that God ordained unto life they found to be unto death. In the Jews' crucifixion of Christ was involved the destruction of Jerusalem. The blood shed upon Calvary was the weight that sank them to ruin for this world and for the world to come. So it will be in the great final day, when judgment shall fall upon the rejecters of God's grace. Christ, their rock of offense, will then appear to them as an avenging mountain. The glory of His countenance, which to the righteous is life, will be to the wicked a consuming fire. Because of love rejected, grace despised, the sinner will be destroyed.

By many illustrations and repeated warnings, Jesus showed what would be the result to the Jews of rejecting the Son of God. In these words He was addressing all in every age who refuse to receive Him as their

Redeemer. Every warning is for them. The desecrated temple, the disobe-dient son, the false husbandmen, the contemptuous builders, have their counterpart in the experience of every sinner. Unless he repent, the doom which they foreshadowed will be his.

12

Controversy

This chapter is based on Matthew 22:15-46; Mark 12:13-40; Luke 20:20-47.

The priests and rulers had listened in silence to Christ's pointed rebukes. They could not refute His charges. But they were only the more determined to entrap Him, and with this object they sent to Him spies, "which should feign themselves just men, that they might take hold of His words, that so they might deliver Him unto the power and authority of the governor." They did not send the old Pharisees whom Jesus had often met, but young men, who were ardent and zealous, and whom, they thought, Christ did not know. These were accompanied by certain of the Herodians, who were to hear Christ's words, that they might testify against Him at His trial. The Pharisees and Herodians had been bitter enemies, but they were now one in enmity to Christ.

The Pharisees had ever chafed under the exaction of tribute by the Romans. The payment of tribute they held to be contrary to the law of God. Now they saw opportunity to lay a snare for Jesus. The spies came to Him, and with apparent sincerity, as though desiring to know their duty, said, "Master, we know that Thou sayest and teachest rightly, neither acceptest Thou the person of any, but teachest the way of God truly: is it lawful for us to give tribute unto Caesar, or no?"

The words, "We know that Thou sayest and teachest rightly," had they been sincere, would have been a wonderful admission. But they were spoken to deceive; nevertheless their testimony was true. The Pharisees did know that Christ said and taught rightly, and by their own testimony will they be judged.

Those who put the question to Jesus thought that they had sufficiently disguised their purpose; but Jesus read their hearts as an open book, and sounded their hypocrisy. "Why tempt ye Me?" He said; thus giving them a sign they had not asked, by showing that He read their hidden purpose. They were still more confused when He added, "Show Me a penny." They brought it, and He asked them, "Whose image and superscription hath it? They answered and said, Caesar's." Pointing to the inscription on the coin, Jesus said, "Render therefore unto Caesar the things which are Caesar's; and unto God the things that are God's."

The spies had expected Jesus to answer their question directly, in one way or the other. If He should say, It is unlawful to give tribute to Caesar,

He would be reported to the Roman authorities and arrested for inciting rebellion. But in case He should pronounce it lawful to pay the tribute, they designed to accuse Him to the people as opposing the law of God. Now they felt themselves baffled and defeated. Their plans were disarranged. The summary manner in which their question had been settled left them nothing further to say.

Christ's reply was no evasion, but a candid answer to the question. Holding in His hand the Roman coin, upon which were stamped the name and image of Caesar, He declared that since they were living under the protection of the Roman power, they should render to that power the support it claimed, so long as this did not conflict with a higher duty. But while peaceably subject to the laws of the land, they should at all times give their first allegiance to God.

The Saviour's words, "Render ... unto God the things that are God's," were a severe rebuke to the intriguing Jews. Had they faithfully fulfilled their obligations to God, they would not have become a broken nation, subject to a foreign power. No Roman ensign would have waved over Jerusalem, no Roman sentinel would have stood at her gates, no Roman governor would have ruled within her walls. The Jewish nation was then paying the penalty of its apostasy from God.

When the Pharisees heard Christ's answer, "they marveled, and left Him, and went their way." He had rebuked their hypocrisy and presumption, and in doing this He had stated a great principle, a principle that clearly defines the limits of man's duty to the civil government and his duty to God. In many minds a vexed question had been settled. Ever after they held to the right principle. And although many went away dissatisfied, they saw that the principle underlying the question had been clearly set forth, and they marveled at Christ's far-seeing discernment.

No sooner were the Pharisees silenced than the Sadducees came forward with their artful questions. The two parties stood in bitter opposition to each other. The Pharisees were rigid adherents to tradition. They were exact in outward ceremonies, diligent in washings, fastings, and long prayers, and ostentatious in almsgiving. But Christ declared that they made void the law of God by teaching for doctrines the commandments of men. As a class they were bigoted and hypocritical; yet among them were persons of genuine piety, who accepted Christ's teachings and became His disciples. The Sadducees rejected the traditions of the Pharisees. They professed to believe the greater portion of the Scriptures, and to regard them as the rule of action; but practically they were skeptics and materialists.

The Sadducees denied the existence of angels, the resurrection of the dead, and the doctrine of a future life, with its rewards and punishments. On all these points they differed with the Pharisees. Between the two parties the resurrection was especially a subject of controversy. The Pharisees had been firm believers in the resurrection, but in these discussions their views in regard to the future state became confused. Death became to them an inexplicable mystery. Their inability to meet the arguments of the Sadducees gave rise to continual irritation. The discussions between the two parties usually resulted in angry disputes, leaving them farther apart than before.

In numbers the Sadducees fell far below their opponents, and they had not so strong a hold upon the common people; but many of them were wealthy, and they had the influence which wealth imparts. In their ranks were included most of the priests, and from among them the high priest was usually chosen. This was, however, with the express stipulation that their skeptical opinions should not be made prominent. On account of the numbers and popularity of the Pharisees, it was necessary for the Sadducees to concede outwardly to their doctrines when holding any priestly office; but the very fact that they were eligible to such office gave influence to their errors.

The Sadducees rejected the teaching of Jesus; He was animated by a spirit which they would not acknowledge as manifesting itself thus; and His teaching in regard to God and the future life contradicted their theories. They believed in God as the only being superior to man; but they argued that an overruling providence and a divine foresight would deprive man of free moral agency, and degrade him to the position of a slave. It was their belief, that, having created man, God had left him to himself, independent of a higher influence. They held that man was free to control his own life and to shape the events of the world; that his destiny was in his own hands. They denied that the Spirit of God works through human efforts or natural means. Yet they still held that, through the proper employment of his natural powers, man could become elevated and enlightened; that by rigorous and austere exactions his life could be purified.

Their ideas of God molded their own character. As in their view He had no interest in man, so they had little regard for one another; there was little union among them. Refusing to acknowledge the influence of the Holy Spirit upon human action, they lacked His power in their lives. Like the rest of the Jews, they boasted much of their birthright as children of Abraham, and of their strict adherence to the requirements of the law; but of the true spirit of the law and the faith and benevolence of Abraham, they were destitute. Their natural sympathies were brought within a narrow compass. They believed it possible for all men to secure the comforts and blessings of life; and their hearts were not touched by the wants and sufferings of others. They lived for themselves.

By His words and His works, Christ testified to a divine power that produces supernatural results, to a future life beyond the present, to God as a Father of the children of men, ever watchful of their true interests. He revealed the working of divine power in benevolence and compassion that rebuked the selfish exclusiveness of the Sadducees. He taught that both for man's temporal and for his eternal good, God moves upon the heart by the Holy Spirit. He showed the error of trusting to human power for that transformation of character which can be wrought only by the Spirit of God.

This teaching the Sadducees were determined to discredit. In seeking a controversy with Jesus, they felt confident of bringing Him into disrepute, even if they could not secure His condemnation. The resurrection was the subject on which they chose to question Him. Should He agree with them, He would give still further offense to the Pharisees. Should He differ with them, they designed to hold His teaching up to ridicule.

The Sadducees reasoned that if the body is to be composed of the same particles of matter in its immortal as in its mortal state, then when raised from the dead it must have flesh and blood, and must resume in the eternal world the life interrupted on earth. In that case they concluded that earthly relationships would be resumed, husband and wife would be reunited, marriages consummated, and all things go on the same as before death, the frailties and passions of this life being perpetuated in the life beyond.

In answer to their questions, Jesus lifted the veil from the future life. "In the resurrection," He said, "they neither marry, nor are given in marriage, but are as the angels of God in heaven." He showed that the Sadducees were wrong in their belief. Their premises were false. "Ye do err," He added, "not knowing the Scriptures, nor the power of God." He did not charge them, as He had charged the Pharisees, with hypocrisy, but with error of belief.

The Sadducees had flattered themselves that they of all men adhered most strictly to the Scriptures. But Jesus showed that they had not known their true meaning. That knowledge must be brought home to the heart by the enlightenment of the Holy Spirit. Their ignorance of the Scriptures and the power of God He declared to be the cause of their confusion of faith and darkness of mind. They were seeking to bring the mysteries of God within the compass of their finite reasoning. Christ called upon them to open their minds to those sacred truths that would broaden and strengthen the understanding. Thousands become infidels because their finite minds cannot comprehend the mysteries of God. They cannot explain the wonderful exhibition of divine power in His providences, therefore they reject the evidences of such power, attributing them to natural agencies which they can comprehend still less. The only key to the mysteries that surround us is to acknowledge in them all the presence and power of God. Men need to recognize God as the Creator of the universe, One who commands and executes all things. They need a broader view of His character, and of the mystery of His agencies.

Christ declared to His hearers that if there were no resurrection of the dead, the Scriptures which they professed to believe would be of no avail. He said, "But as touching the resurrection of the dead, have ye not read that which was spoken unto you by God, saying, I am the God of Abraham, and the God of Isaac, and the God of Jacob? God is not the God of the dead, but of the living." God counts the things that are not as though they were. He sees the end from the beginning, and beholds the result of His work as though it were now accomplished. The precious dead, from Adam down to the last saint who dies, will hear the voice of the Son of God, and will come forth from the grave to immortal life. God will be their God, and they shall be His people. There will be a close and tender relationship between God and the risen saints. This condition, which is anticipated in His purpose, He beholds as if it were already existing. The dead live unto Him.

By the words of Christ the Sadducees were put to silence. They could not answer Him. Not a word had been spoken of which the least advantage could be taken for His condemnation. His adversaries had gained nothing but the contempt of the people.

The Pharisees, however, did not yet despair of driving Him to speak that which they could use against Him. They prevailed upon a certain learned scribe to question Jesus as to which of the ten precepts of the law was of the greatest importance.

The Pharisees had exalted the first four commandments, which point out the duty of man to his Maker, as of far greater consequence than the other six, which define man's duty to his fellow man. As the result, they greatly failed of practical godliness. Jesus had shown the people their great deficiency, and had taught the necessity of good works, declaring that the tree is known by its fruits. For this reason He had been charged with exalting the last six commandments above the first four.

The lawyer approached Jesus with a direct question, "Which is the first commandment of all?" The answer of Christ is direct and forcible: "The first of all the commandments is, Hear, O Israel; The Lord our God is one Lord: and thou shalt love the Lord thy God with all thy heart, and with all thy soul, and with all thy mind, and with all thy strength: this is the first commandment." The second is like the first, said Christ; for it flows out of it, "Thou shalt love thy neighbor as thyself. There is none other commandment greater than these." "On these two commandments hang all the law and the prophets."

The first four of the Ten Commandments are summed up in the one great precept, "Thou shalt love the Lord thy God with all thy heart." The last six are included in the other, "Thou shalt love thy neighbor as thyself." Both these commandments are an expression of the principle of love. The first cannot be kept and the second broken, nor can the second be kept while the first is broken. When God has His rightful place on the throne of the heart, the right place will be given to our neighbor. We shall love him as ourselves. And only as we love God supremely is it possible to love our neighbor impartially.

And since all the commandments are summed up in love to God and man, it follows that not one precept can be broken without violating this principle. Thus Christ taught His hearers that the law of God is not so many separate precepts, some of which are of great importance, while others are of small importance and may with impunity be ignored. Our Lord presents the first four and the last six commandments as a divine whole, and teaches that love to God will be shown by obedience to all His commandments.

The scribe who had questioned Jesus was well read in the law, and he was astonished at His words. He did not expect Him to manifest so deep and thorough a knowledge of the Scriptures. He had gained a broader view of the principles underlying the sacred precepts. Before the assembled priests and rulers he honestly acknowledged that Christ had given the right interpretation to the law, saying:

"Well, Master, Thou hast said the truth: for there is one God; and there is none other but He: and to love Him with all the heart, and with all the understanding, and with all the soul, and with all the strength, and to love his neighbor as himself, is more than all whole burnt offerings and sacrifices."

The wisdom of Christ's answer had convicted the scribe. He knew that the Jewish religion consisted in outward ceremonies rather than inward piety. He had some sense of the worthlessness of mere ceremonial offerings, and the faithless shedding of blood for expiation of sin. Love and obedience to God, and unselfish regard for man, appeared to him of more value than all these rites. The readiness of this man to acknowledge the correctness of Christ's reasoning, and his decided and prompt response before the people, manifested a spirit entirely different from that of the priests and rulers. The heart of Jesus went out in pity to the honest scribe who had dared to face the frowns of the priests and the threats of the rulers to speak the convictions of his heart. "And when Jesus saw that he answered discreetly, He said unto him, Thou art not far from the kingdom of God."

The scribe was near to the kingdom of God, in that he recognized deeds of righteousness as more acceptable to God than burnt offerings and sacrifices. But he needed to recognize the divine character of Christ, and through faith in Him receive power to do the works of righteousness. The ritual service was of no value, unless connected with Christ by living faith. Even the moral law fails of its purpose, unless it is understood in its relation to the Saviour. Christ had repeatedly shown that His Father's law contained something deeper than mere authoritative commands. In the law is embodied the same principle that is revealed in the gospel. The law points out man's duty and shows him his guilt. To Christ he must look for pardon and for power to do what the law enjoins.

The Pharisees had gathered close about Jesus as He answered the question of the scribe. Now turning He put a question to them: "What think ye of Christ? whose son is He?" This question was designed to test their belief concerning the Messiah,—to show whether they regarded Him simply as a man or as the Son of God. A chorus of voices answered, "The Son of David." This was the title which prophecy had given to the Messiah. When Jesus revealed His divinity by His mighty miracles, when He healed the sick and raised the dead, the people had inquired among themselves, "Is not this the Son of David?" The Syrophoenician woman, blind Bartimaeus, and many others had cried to Him for help, "Have mercy on me, O Lord, Thou Son of David." Matt. 15:22. While riding into Jerusalem He had been hailed with the joyful shout, "Hosanna to the Son of David: Blessed is He that cometh in the name of the Lord." Matt. 21:9. And the little children in the temple had that day echoed the glad ascription. But many who called Jesus the Son of David did not recognize His divinity. They did not understand that the Son of David was also the Son of God.

In reply to the statement that Christ was the Son of David, Jesus said, "How then doth David in Spirit [the Spirit of Inspiration from God] call Him Lord, saying, The Lord said unto my Lord, Sit Thou on My right hand, till I make Thine enemies Thy footstool? If David then call Him Lord, how is He his son? And no man was able to answer Him a word, neither durst any man from that day forth ask Him any more questions."

13

Woes on the Pharisees

This chapter is based on Matthew 23; Mark 12:41-44; Luke 20:45-47; 21:1-4.

It was the last day of Christ's teaching in the temple. Of the vast throngs that were gathered at Jerusalem, the attention of all had been attracted to Him; the people had crowded the temple courts, watching the contest that had been in progress, and they eagerly caught every word that fell from His lips. Never before had such a scene been witnessed. There stood the young Galilean, bearing no earthly honor or royal badge. Surrounding Him were priests in their rich apparel, rulers with robes and badges significant of their exalted station, and scribes with scrolls in their hands, to which they made frequent reference. Jesus stood calmly before them, with the dignity of a king. As one invested with the authority of heaven, He looked unflinchingly upon His adversaries, who had rejected and despised His teachings, and who thirsted for His life. They had assailed Him in great numbers, but their schemes to ensnare and condemn Him had been in vain. Challenge after challenge He had met, presenting the pure, bright truth in contrast to the darkness and errors of the priests and Pharisees. He had set before these leaders their real condition, and the retribution sure to follow persistence in their evil deeds. The warning had been faithfully given. Yet another work remained for Christ to do. Another purpose was still to be accomplished.

The interest of the people in Christ and His work had steadily increased. They were charmed with His teaching, but they were also greatly perplexed. They had respected the priests and rabbis for their intelligence and apparent piety. In all religious matters they had ever yielded implicit obedience to their authority. Yet they now saw these men trying to cast discredit upon Jesus, a teacher whose virtue and knowledge shone forth the brighter from every assault. They looked upon the lowering countenances of the priests and elders, and there saw discomfiture and confusion. They marveled that the rulers would not believe on Jesus, when His teachings were so plain and simple. They themselves knew not what course to take. With eager anxiety they watched the movements of those whose counsel they had always followed.

In the parables which Christ had spoken, it was His purpose both to warn the rulers and to instruct the people who were willing to be taught. But there was need to speak yet more plainly. Through their reverence for tradition and their blind faith in a corrupt priesthood, the people were enslaved. These chains Christ must break. The character of the priests, rulers, and Pharisees must be more fully exposed.

"The scribes and the Pharisees," He said, "sit in Moses' seat: all therefore whatsoever they bid you observe, that observe and do; but do not ye after their works: for they say, and do not." The scribes and Pharisees claimed to be invested with divine authority similar to that of Moses. They assumed to take his place as expounders of the law and judges of the people. As such they claimed from the people the utmost deference and obedience. Jesus bade His hearers do that which the rabbis taught according to the law, but not to follow their example. They themselves did not practice their own teaching.

And they taught much that was contrary to the Scriptures. Jesus said, "They bind heavy burdens and grievous to be borne, and lay them on men's shoulders; but they themselves will not move them with one of their fingers." The Pharisees enjoined a multitude of regulations, having their foundation in tradition, and unreasonably restricting personal liberty. And certain portions of the law they so explained as to impose upon the people observances which they themselves secretly ignored, and from which, when it served their purpose, they actually claimed exemption.

To make a show of their piety was their constant aim. Nothing was held too sacred to serve this end. To Moses God had said concerning His commandments, "Thou shalt bind them for a sign upon thine hand, and they shall be as frontlets between thine eyes." Deut. 6:8. These words have a deep meaning. As the word of God is meditated upon and practiced, the whole man will be ennobled. In righteous and merciful dealing, the hands will reveal, as a signet, the principles of God's law. They will be kept clean from bribes, and from all that is corrupt and deceptive. They will be active in works of love and compassion. The eyes, directed toward a noble purpose, will be clear and true. The expressive countenance, the speaking eye, will testify to the blameless character of him who loves and honors the word of God. But by the Jews of Christ's day all this was undiscerned. The command given to Moses was construed into a direction that the precepts of Scripture should be worn upon the person. They were accordingly written upon strips of parchment, and bound in a conspicuous manner about the head and wrists. But this did not cause the law of God to take a firmer hold of the mind and heart. These parchments were worn merely as badges, to attract attention. They were thought to give the wearers an air of devotion which would command the reverence of the people. Jesus struck a blow at this vain pretense:

"But all their works they do for to be seen of men: they make broad their phylacteries, and enlarge the borders of their garments, and love the uppermost rooms at feasts, and the chief seats in the synagogues, and greetings in the markets, and to be called of men, Rabbi, Rabbi. But be not ye called Rabbi: for one is your Master, even Christ; and all ye are brethren. And call no man your father upon the earth: for One is your Father, which is in heaven. Neither be ye called master: for One is your Master, even Christ." In such plain words the Saviour revealed the selfish ambition that was ever reaching for place and power, displaying a mock humility, while the heart was filled with avarice and envy. When persons were invited to a feast, the guests were seated according to their rank, and those who were given the most honorable place received the first attention and special favors. The Pharisees were ever scheming to secure these honors. This practice Jesus rebuked.

He also reproved the vanity shown in coveting the title of rabbi, or master. Such a title, He declared, belonged not to men, but to Christ. Priests, scribes, and rulers, expounders and administrators of the law, were all brethren, children of one Father. Jesus impressed upon the people that they were to give no man a title of honor indicating his control of their conscience or their faith.

If Christ were on earth today, surrounded by those who bear the title of "Reverend" or "Right Reverend," would He not repeat His saying, "Neither be ye called masters: for One is your Master, even Christ"? The Scripture declares of God, "Holy and reverend is His name." Ps. 111:9. To what human being is such a title befitting? How little does man reveal of the wisdom and righteousness it indicates! How many of those who assume this title are misrepresenting the name and character of God! Alas, how often have worldly ambition, despotism, and the basest sins been hidden under the broidered garments of a high and holy office! The Saviour continued:

"But he that is greatest among you shall be your servant. And whosoever shall exalt himself shall be abased; and he that shall humble himself shall be exalted." Again and again Christ had taught that true greatness is measured by moral worth. In the estimation of heaven, greatness of character consists in living for the welfare of our fellow men, in doing works of love and mercy. Christ the King of glory was a servant to fallen man.

"Woe unto you, scribes and Pharisees, hypocrites," said Jesus; "for ye shut up the kingdom of heaven against men: for ye neither go in yourselves, neither suffer ye them that are entering to go in." By perverting the Scriptures, the priests and lawyers blinded the minds of those who would otherwise have received a knowledge of Christ's kingdom, and that inward, divine life which is essential to true holiness.

"Woe unto you, scribes and Pharisees, hypocrites! for ye devour widows' houses, and for a pretense make long prayer: therefore ye shall receive the greater damnation." The Pharisees had great influence with the people, and of this they took advantage to serve their own interests. They gained the confidence of pious widows, and then represented it as a duty for them to devote their property to religious purposes. Having secured control of their money, the wily schemers used it for their own benefit. To cover their dishonesty, they offered long prayers in public, and made a great show of piety. This hypocrisy Christ declared would bring them the greater damnation. The same rebuke falls upon many in our day who make a high profession of piety. Their lives are stained by selfishness and avarice, yet they throw over it all a garment of seeming purity, and thus for a time deceive their fellow men. But they cannot deceive God. He reads every purpose of the heart, and will judge every man according to his deeds.

Christ unsparingly condemned abuses, but He was careful not to lessen obligation. He rebuked the selfishness that extorted and misapplied the widow's gifts. At the same time He commended the widow who brought her offering for God's treasury. Man's abuse of the gift could not turn God's blessing from the giver.

Jesus was in the court where were the treasure chests, and He watched those who came to deposit their gifts. Many of the rich brought large sums, which they presented with great ostentation. Jesus looked upon them sadly, but made no comment on their liberal offerings. Presently His countenance lighted as He saw a poor widow approach hesitatingly, as though fearful of being observed. As the rich and haughty swept by, to deposit their offerings, she shrank back as if hardly daring to venture farther. And yet she longed to do something, little though it might be, for the cause she loved. She looked at the gift in her hand. It was very small in comparison with the gifts of those around her, yet it was her all. Watching her opportunity, she hurriedly threw in her two mites, and turned to hasten away. But in doing this she caught the eye of Jesus, which was fastened earnestly upon her.

The Saviour called His disciples to Him, and bade them mark the widow's poverty. Then His words of commendation fell upon her ear: "Of a truth I say unto you, that this poor widow hath cast in more than they all." Tears of joy filled her eyes as she felt that her act was understood and appreciated. Many would have advised her to keep her pittance for her own use; given into the hands of the well-fed priests, it would be lost sight of among the many costly gifts brought to the treasury. But Jesus understood her motive. She believed the service of the temple to be of God's appointment, and she was anxious to do her utmost to sustain it. She did what she could, and her act was to be a monument to her memory through all time, and her joy in eternity. Her heart went with her gift; its value was estimated, not by the worth of the coin, but by the love to God and the interest in His work that had prompted the deed.

Jesus said of the poor widow, She "hath cast in more than they all." The rich had bestowed from their abundance, many of them to be seen and honored by men. Their large donations had deprived them of no comfort, or even luxury; they had required no sacrifice, and could not be compared in value with the widow's mite.

It is the motive that gives character to our acts, stamping them with ignominy or with high moral worth. Not the great things which every eye sees and every tongue praises does God account most precious. The little duties cheerfully done, the little gifts which make no show, and which to human eyes may appear worthless, often stand highest in His sight. A heart of faith and love is dearer to God than the most costly gift. The poor widow gave her living to do the little that she did. She deprived herself of food in order to give those two mites to the cause she loved. And she did it in faith, believing that her heavenly Father would not overlook her great need. It was this unselfish spirit and childlike faith that won the Saviour's commendation.

Among the poor there are many who long to show their gratitude to God for His grace and truth. They greatly desire to share with their more prosperous brethren in sustaining His service. These souls should not be repulsed. Let them lay up their mites in the bank of heaven. If given from a heart filled with love for God, these seeming trifles become consecrated gifts, priceless offerings, which God smiles upon and blesses.

When Jesus said of the widow, She "hath cast in more than they all," His words were true, not only of the motive, but of the results of her gift. The "two mites which make a farthing" have brought to God's treasury an amount of money far greater than the contributions of those rich Jews. The influence of that little gift has been like a stream, small in its beginning, but widening and deepening as it flowed down through the ages. In a thousand ways it has contributed to the relief of the poor and the spread of the gospel. Her example of self-sacrifice has acted and reacted upon thousands of hearts in every land and in every age. It has appealed to both the rich and the poor, and their offerings have swelled the value of her gift. God's blessing upon the widow's mite has made it the source of great results. So with every gift bestowed and every act performed with a sincere desire for God's glory. It is linked with the purposes of Omnipotence. Its results for good no man can measure.

The Saviour continued His denunciations of the scribes and Pharisees: "Woe unto you, ye blind guides, which say, Whosoever shall swear by the temple, it is nothing; but whosoever shall swear by the gold of the temple, he is a debtor! Ye fools and blind: for whether is greater, the gold, or the temple that sanctifieth the gold? and, Whosoever shall swear by the altar, it is nothing; but whosoever sweareth by the gift that is upon it, he is guilty. Ye fools and blind: for whether is greater, the gift, or the altar that sanctifieth the gift?" The priests interpreted God's requirements according to their own false and narrow standard. They presumed to make nice distinctions as to the comparative guilt of various sins, passing over some lightly, and treating others of perhaps less consequence as unpardonable. For a money consideration they excused persons from their vows. And for large sums of money they sometimes passed over aggravated crimes. At the same time these priests and rulers would in other cases pronounce severe judgment for trivial offenses.

"Woe unto you, scribes and Pharisees, hypocrites! for ye pay tithe of mint and anise and cummin, and have omitted the weightier matters of the law, judgment, mercy, and faith: these ought ye to have done, and not to leave the other undone." In these words Christ again condemns the abuse of sacred obligation. The obligation itself He does not set aside. The tithing system was ordained by God, and it had been observed from the earliest times. Abraham, the father of the faithful, paid tithes of all that he possessed. The Jewish rulers recognized the obligation of tithing, and this was right; but they did not leave the people to carry out their own convictions of duty. Arbitrary rules were laid down for every case. The requirements had become so complicated that it was impossible for them to be fulfilled. None knew when their obligations were met. As God gave it, the system was just and reasonable; but the priests and rabbis had made it a wearisome burden.

All that God commands is of consequence. Christ recognized the payment of tithes as a duty; but He showed that this could not excuse the neglect of other duties. The Pharisees were very exact in tithing garden herbs, such as mint, anise, and rue; this cost them little, and it gave them a reputation for exactness and sanctity. At the same time their useless restrictions oppressed the people and destroyed respect for the sacred system of God's own appointing. They occupied men's minds with trifling distinctions, and turned their attention from essential truths. The weightier matters of the law, justice, mercy, and truth, were neglected. "These," Christ said, "ought ye to have done, and not to leave the other undone."

Other laws had been perverted by the rabbis in like manner. In the directions given through Moses it was forbidden to eat any unclean thing. The use of swine's flesh, and the flesh of certain other animals, was prohibited, as likely to fill the blood with impurities, and to shorten life. But the Pharisees did not leave these restrictions as God had given them. They went to unwarranted extremes. Among other things the people were required to strain all the water used, lest it should contain the smallest insect, which might be classed with the unclean animals. Jesus, contrasting these trivial exactions with the magnitude of their actual sins, said to the Pharisees, "Ye blind guides, which strain at a gnat, and swallow a camel."

"Woe unto you, scribes and Pharisees, hypocrites! for ye are like unto whited sepulchers, which indeed appear beautiful outward, but are within full of dead men's bones, and of all uncleanness." As the whited and beautifully decorated tomb concealed the putrefying remains within, so the outward holiness of the priests and rulers concealed iniquity. Jesus continued:

"Woe unto you, scribes and Pharisees, hypocrites! because ye build the tombs of the prophets, and garnish the sepulchers of the righteous, and say, If we had been in the days of our fathers, we would not have been partakers with them in the blood of the prophets. Wherefore ye be witnesses unto yourselves, that ye are the children of them which killed the prophets." To show their esteem for the dead prophets, the Jews were very zealous in beautifying their tombs; but they did not profit by their teachings, nor give heed to their reproofs.

In the days of Christ a superstitious regard was cherished for the resting places of the dead, and vast sums of money were lavished upon their decoration. In the sight of God this was idolatry. In their undue regard for the dead, men showed that they did not love God supremely, nor their neighbor as themselves. The same idolatry is carried to great lengths today. Many are guilty of neglecting the widow and the fatherless, the sick and the poor, in order to build expensive monuments for the dead. Time, money, and labor are freely spent for this purpose, while duties to the living—duties which Christ has plainly enjoined—are left undone.

The Pharisees built the tombs of the prophets, and adorned their sepulchers, and said one to another, If we had lived in the days of our fathers, we would not have united with them in shedding the blood of God's servants. At the same time they were planning to take the life of His Son. This should be a lesson to us. It should open our eyes to the power of Satan to deceive the mind that turns from the light of truth. Many follow in the track of the Pharisees. They revere those who have died for their faith. They wonder at the blindness of the Jews in rejecting Christ. Had we lived in His day, they declare, we would gladly have received His teaching; we would never have been partakers in the guilt of those who rejected the Saviour. But when obedience to God requires self-denial and humiliation, these very persons stifle their convictions, and refuse obedience. Thus they manifest the same spirit as did the Pharisees whom Christ condemned.

Little did the Jews realize the terrible responsibility involved in rejecting Christ. From the time when the first innocent blood was shed, when righteous Abel fell by the hand of Cain, the same history had been repeated, with increasing guilt. In every age prophets had lifted up their voices against the sins of kings, rulers, and people, speaking the words which God gave them, and obeying His will at the peril of their lives. From generation to generation there had been heaping up a terrible punishment for the rejecters of light and truth. This the enemies of Christ were now drawing down upon their own heads. The sin of the priests and rulers was greater than that of any preceding generation. By their rejection of the Saviour, they were making themselves responsible for the blood of all the righteous men slain from Abel to Christ. They were about to fill to overflowing their cup of iniquity. And soon it was to be poured upon their heads in retributive justice. Of this, Jesus warned them:

"That upon you may come all the righteous blood shed upon the earth, from the blood of righteous Abel unto the blood of Zacharias son of Barachias, whom ye slew between the temple and the altar. Verily I say unto you, All these things shall come upon this generation."

The scribes and Pharisees who listened to Jesus knew that His words were true. They knew how the prophet Zacharias had been slain. While the words of warning from God were upon his lips, a satanic fury seized the apostate king, and at his command the prophet was put to death. His blood had imprinted itself upon the very stones of the temple court, and could not be erased; it remained to bear testimony against apostate Israel. As long as the temple should stand, there would be the stain of that righteous blood, crying to God to be avenged. As Jesus referred to these fearful sins, a thrill of horror ran through the multitude.

Looking forward, Jesus declared that the impenitence of the Jews and their intolerance of God's servants would be the same in the future as it had been in the past:

"Wherefore, behold, I send unto you prophets, and wise men, and scribes: and some of them ye shall kill and crucify; and some of them shall ye scourge in your synagogues, and persecute them from city to city." Prophets and wise men, full of faith and the Holy Ghost,—Stephen, James, and many others,—would be condemned and slain. With hand uplifted to heaven, and a divine light enshrouding His person, Christ spoke as a judge to those before Him. His voice, that had so often been heard in gentleness and entreaty, was now heard in rebuke and condemnation. The listeners shuddered. Never was the impression made by His words and His look to be effaced.

Christ's indignation was directed against the hypocrisy, the gross sins, by which men were destroying their own souls, deceiving the people and dishonoring God. In the specious deceptive reasoning of the priests and rulers He discerned the working of satanic agencies. Keen and searching had been His denunciation of sin; but He spoke no words of retaliation. He had a holy wrath against the prince of darkness; but He manifested no irritated temper. So the Christian who lives in harmony with God, possessing the sweet attributes of love and mercy, will feel a righteous indignation against sin; but he will not be roused by passion to revile those who revile him. Even in meeting those who are moved by a power from beneath to maintain falsehood, in Christ he will still preserve calmness and self-possession.

Divine pity marked the countenance of the Son of God as He cast one lingering look upon the temple and then upon His hearers. In a voice choked by deep anguish of heart and bitter tears He exclaimed, "O Jerusalem, Jerusalem, thou that killest the prophets, and stonest them which are sent unto thee, how often would I have gathered thy children together, even as a hen gathereth her chickens under her wings, and ye would not!" This is the separation struggle. In the lamentation of Christ the very heart of God is pouring itself forth. It is the mysterious farewell of the long-suffering love of the Deity.

Pharisees and Sadducees were alike silenced. Jesus summoned His disciples, and prepared to leave the temple, not as one defeated and forced from the presence of his adversaries, but as one whose work was accomplished. He retired a victor from the contest.

The gems of truth that fell from Christ's lips on that eventful day were treasured in many hearts. For them new thoughts started into life, new aspirations were awakened, and a new history began. After the crucifixion and resurrection of Christ, these persons came to the front, and fulfilled their divine commission with a wisdom and zeal corresponding to the greatness of the work. They bore a message that appealed to the hearts of men, weakening the old superstitions that had long dwarfed the lives of thousands. Before their testimony human theories and philosophies became as idle fables. Mighty were the results flowing from the words of the Saviour to that wondering, awestruck crowd in the temple at Jerusalem.

But Israel as a nation had divorced herself from God. The natural branches of the olive tree were broken off. Looking for the last time upon the interior of the temple, Jesus said with mournful pathos, "Behold, your house is left unto you desolate. For I say unto you, Ye shall not see Me henceforth, till ye shall say, Blessed is He that cometh in the name of the Lord." Hitherto He had called the temple His Father's house; but now, as the Son of God should pass out from those walls, God's presence would be withdrawn forever from the temple built to His glory. Henceforth its ceremonies would be meaningless, its services a mockery.

14

"The Least of These My Brethren"

This chapter is based on Matthew 25:31-46.

"When the Son of man shall come in His glory, and all the holy angels with Him, then shall He sit upon the throne of His glory: and before Him shall be gathered all nations: and He shall separate them one from another." Thus Christ on the Mount of Olives pictured to His disciples the scene of the great judgment day. And He represented its decision as turning upon one point. When the nations are gathered before Him, there will be but two classes, and their eternal destiny will be determined by what they have done or have neglected to do for Him in the person of the poor and the suffering.

In that day Christ does not present before men the great work He has done for them in giving His life for their redemption. He presents the faithful work they have done for Him. To those whom He sets upon His right hand He will say, "Come, ye blessed of My Father, inherit the kingdom prepared for you from the foundation of the world: for I was an hungered, and ye gave Me meat: I was thirsty, and ye gave Me drink: I was a stranger, and ye took Me in: naked, and ye clothed Me: I was sick, and ye visited Me: I was in prison, and ye came unto Me." But those whom Christ commends know not that they have been ministering unto Him. To their perplexed inquiries He answers, "Inasmuch as ye have done it unto one of the least of these My brethren, ye have done it unto Me."

Jesus had told His disciples that they were to be hated of all men, to be persecuted and afflicted. Many would be driven from their homes, and brought to poverty. Many would be in distress through disease and privation. Many would be cast into prison. To all who forsook friends or home for His sake He had promised in this life a hundredfold. Now He assured a special blessing to all who should minister to their brethren. In all who suffer for My name, said Jesus, you are to recognize Me. As you would minister to Me, so you are to minister to them. This is the evidence that you are My disciples.

All who have been born into the heavenly family are in a special sense the brethren of our Lord. The love of Christ binds together the members of His family, and wherever that love is made manifest there the divine relationship is revealed. "Everyone that loveth is born of God, and knoweth God." 1 John 4:7.

Those whom Christ commends in the judgment may have known little of theology, but they have cherished His principles. Through the influence of the divine Spirit they have been a blessing to those about them. Even among the heathen are those who have cherished the spirit of kindness; before the words of life had fallen upon their ears, they have befriended the missionaries, even ministering to them at the peril of their own lives. Among the heathen are those who worship God ignorantly, those to whom the light is never brought by human instrumentality, yet they will not perish. Though ignorant of the written law of God, they have heard His voice speaking to them in nature, and have done the things that the law required. Their works are evidence that the Holy Spirit has touched their hearts, and they are recognized as the children of God.

How surprised and gladdened will be the lowly among the nations, and among the heathen, to hear from the lips of the Saviour, "Inasmuch as ye have done it unto one of the least of these My brethren, ye have done it unto Me!" How glad will be the heart of Infinite Love as His followers look up with surprise and joy at His words of approval!

But not to any class is Christ's love restricted. He identifies Himself with every child of humanity. That we might become members of the heavenly family, He became a member of the earthly family. He is the Son of man, and thus a brother to every son and daughter of Adam. His followers are not to feel themselves detached from the perishing world around them. They are a part of the great web of humanity; and Heaven looks upon them as brothers to sinners as well as to saints. The fallen, the erring, and the sinful, Christ's love embraces; and every deed of kindness done to uplift a fallen soul, every act of mercy, is accepted as done to Him.

The angels of heaven are sent forth to minister to those who shall be heirs of salvation. We know not now who they are; it is not yet made manifest who shall overcome, and share the inheritance of the saints in light; but angels of heaven are passing throughout the length and breadth of the earth, seeking to comfort the sorrowing, to protect the imperiled, to win the hearts of men to Christ. Not one is neglected or passed by. God is no respecter of persons, and He has an equal care for all the souls He has created.

As you open your door to Christ's needy and suffering ones, you are welcoming unseen angels. You invite the companionship of heavenly beings. They bring a sacred atmosphere of joy and peace. They come with praises upon their lips, and an answering strain is heard in heaven. Every deed of mercy makes music there. The Father from His throne numbers the unselfish workers among His most precious treasures.

Those on the left hand of Christ, those who had neglected Him in the person of the poor and the suffering, were unconscious of their guilt. Satan had blinded them; they had not perceived what they owed to their brethren. They had been self-absorbed, and cared not for others' needs.

To the rich, God has given wealth that they may relieve and comfort His suffering children; but too often they are indifferent to the wants of others. They feel themselves superior to their poor brethren. They do not put themselves in the poor man's place. They do not understand the temptations and struggles of the poor, and mercy dies out of their hearts. In costly dwellings and splendid churches, the rich shut themselves away from the poor; the means that God has given to bless the needy is spent in pampering pride and selfishness. The poor are robbed daily of the education they should have concerning the tender mercies of God; for He has made ample provision that they should be comforted with the necessities of life. They are compelled to feel the poverty that narrows life, and are often tempted to become envious, jealous, and full of evil surmisings. Those who themselves have not endured the pressure of want too often treat the poor in a contemptuous way, and make them feel that they are looked upon as paupers.

But Christ beholds it all, and He says, It was I who was hungry and thirsty. It was I who was a stranger. It was I who was sick. It was I who was in prison. While you were feasting at your bountifully spread table, I was famishing in the hovel or the empty street. While you were at ease in your luxurious home, I had not where to lay My head. While you crowded your wardrobe with rich apparel, I was destitute. While you pursued your pleasures, I languished in prison.

When you doled out the pittance of bread to the starving poor, when you gave those flimsy garments to shield them from the biting frost, did you remember that you were giving to the Lord of glory? All the days of your life I was near you in the person of these afflicted ones, but you did not seek Me. You would not enter into fellowship with Me. I know you not.

Many feel that it would be a great privilege to visit the scenes of Christ's life on earth, to walk where He trod, to look upon the lake beside which He loved to teach, and the hills and valleys on which His eyes so often rested. But we need not go to Nazareth, to Capernaum, or to Bethany, in order to walk in the steps of Jesus. We shall find His footprints beside the sickbed, in the hovels of poverty, in the crowded alleys of the great city, and in every place where there are human hearts in need of consolation. In doing as Jesus did when on earth, we shall walk in His steps.

All may find something to do. "The poor always ye have with you," (John 12:8), Jesus said, and none need feel that there is no place where they can labor for Him. Millions upon millions of human souls ready to perish, bound in chains of ignorance and sin, have never so much as heard of Christ's love for them. Were our condition and theirs to be reversed, what would we desire them to do for us? All this, so far as lies in our power, we are under the most solemn obligation to do for them. Christ's rule of life, by which every one of us must stand or fall in the judgment, is, "Whatsoever ye would that men should do to you, do ye even so to them." Matt. 7:12.

The Saviour has given His precious life in order to establish a church capable of caring for sorrowful, tempted souls. A company of believers may be poor, uneducated, and unknown; yet in Christ they may do a work in the home, the neighborhood, the church, and even in "the regions beyond," whose results shall be as far-reaching as eternity.

It is because this work is neglected that so many young disciples never advance beyond the mere alphabet of Christian experience. The light which was glowing in their own hearts when Jesus spoke to them, "Thy sins be forgiven thee," they might have kept alive by helping those in need. The restless energy that is so often a source of danger to the young might be directed into channels through which it would flow out in streams of blessing. Self would be forgotten in earnest work to do others good.

Those who minister to others will be ministered unto by the Chief Shepherd. They themselves will drink of the living water, and will be satisfied. They will not be longing for exciting amusements, or for some change in their lives. The great topic of interest will be, how to save the souls that are ready to perish. Social intercourse will be profitable. The love of the Redeemer will draw hearts together in unity.

When we realize that we are workers together with God, His promises will not be spoken with indifference. They will burn in our hearts, and kindle upon our lips. To Moses, when called to minister to an ignorant, undisciplined, and rebellious people, God gave the promise, "My presence shall go with thee, and I will give thee rest." And He said, "Certainly I will be with thee." Ex. 33:14; 3:12. This promise is to all who labor in Christ's stead for His afflicted and suffering ones.

Love to man is the earthward manifestation of the love of God. It was to implant this love, to make us children of one family, that the King of glory became one with us. And when His parting words are fulfilled, "Love one another, as I have loved you" (John 15:12); when we love the world as He has loved it, then for us His mission is accomplished. We are fitted for heaven; for we have heaven in our hearts.

But "if thou forbear to deliver them that are drawn unto death, and those that are ready to be slain; if thou sayest, Behold, we knew it not; doth not He that pondereth the heart consider it? and He that keepeth thy soul, doth not He know it? and shall not He render to every man according to his works?" Prov. 24:11, 12. In the great Judgment day, those who have not worked for Christ, who have drifted along thinking of themselves, caring for themselves, will be placed by the Judge of the whole earth with those who did evil. They receive the same condemnation.

To every soul a trust is given. Of everyone the Chief Shepherd will demand, "Where is the flock that was given thee, thy beautiful flock?" And "what wilt thou say when He shall punish thee?" Jer. 13:20, 21.

15

A Servant of Servants

This chapter is based on Luke 22:7-18, 24; John 13:1-17.

In the upper chamber of a dwelling at Jerusalem, Christ was sitting at table with His disciples. They had gathered to celebrate the Passover. The Saviour desired to keep this feast alone with the twelve. He knew that His hour was come; He Himself was the true paschal lamb, and on the day the Passover was eaten He was to be sacrificed. He was about to drink the cup of wrath; He must soon receive the final baptism of suffering. But a few quiet hours yet remained to Him, and these were to be spent for the benefit of His beloved disciples.

The whole life of Christ had been a life of unselfish service. "Not to be ministered unto, but to minister," (Matt. 20:28), had been the lesson of His every act. But not yet had the disciples learned the lesson. At this last Passover supper, Jesus repeated His teaching by an illustration that impressed it forever on their minds and hearts.

The interviews between Jesus and His disciples were usually seasons of calm joy, highly prized by them all. The Passover suppers had been scenes of special interest; but upon this occasion Jesus was troubled. His heart was burdened, and a shadow rested upon His countenance. As He met the disciples in the upper chamber, they perceived that something weighed heavily upon His mind, and although they knew not its cause, they sympathized with His grief.

As they were gathered about the table, He said in tones of touching sadness, "With desire I have desired to eat this Passover with you before I suffer: for I say unto you, I will not any more eat thereof, until it be fulfilled in the kingdom of God. And He took the cup, and gave thanks, and said, Take this, and divide it among yourselves: for I say unto you, I will not drink of the fruit of the vine, until the kingdom of God shall come."

Christ knew that the time had come for Him to depart out of the world, and go to His Father. And having loved His own that were in the world, He loved them unto the end. He was now in the shadow of the cross, and the pain was torturing His heart. He knew that He would be deserted in the hour of His betrayal. He knew that by the most humiliating process to which criminals were subjected He would be put to death. He knew the ingratitude and cruelty of those He had come to save. He knew how great the sacrifice that He must make, and for how many it would be in vain. Knowing all that was before Him, He might naturally have been overwhelmed with the thought of His own humiliation and suffering. But He looked upon the twelve, who had been with Him as His own, and who, after His shame and sorrow and painful usage were over, would be left to struggle in the world. His thoughts of what He Himself must suffer were ever connected with His disciples. He did not think of Himself. His care for them was uppermost in His mind.

On this last evening with His disciples, Jesus had much to tell them. If they had been prepared to receive what He longed to impart, they would have been saved from heartbreaking anguish, from disappointment and unbelief. But Jesus saw that they could not bear what He had to say. As He looked into their faces, the words of warning and comfort were stayed upon His lips. Moments passed in silence. Jesus appeared to be waiting. The disciples were ill at ease. The sympathy and tenderness awakened by Christ's grief seemed to have passed away. His sorrowful words, pointing to His own suffering, had made little impression. The glances they cast upon each other told of jealousy and contention.

There was "a strife among them, which of them should be accounted the greatest." This contention, carried on in the presence of Christ, grieved and wounded Him. The disciples clung to their favorite idea that Christ would assert His power, and take His position on the throne of David. And in heart each still longed for the highest place in the kingdom. They had placed their own estimate upon themselves and upon one another, and, instead of regarding their brethren as more worthy, they had placed themselves first. The request of James and John to sit on the right and left of Christ's throne had excited the indignation of the others. That the two brothers should presume to ask for the highest position so stirred the ten that alienation threatened. They felt that they were misjudged, that their fidelity and talents were not appreciated. Judas was the most severe upon James and John.

When the disciples entered the supper room, their hearts were full of resentful feelings. Judas pressed next to Christ on the left side; John was on the right. If there was a highest place, Judas was determined to have it, and that place was thought to be next to Christ. And Judas was a traitor.

Another cause of dissension had arisen. At a feast it was customary for a servant to wash the feet of the guests, and on this occasion preparation had been made for the service. The pitcher, the basin, and the towel were there, in readiness for the feet washing; but no servant was present, and it was the disciples' part to perform it. But each of the disciples, yielding to wounded pride, determined not to act the part of a servant. All manifested a stoical unconcern, seeming unconscious that there was anything for them to do. By their silence they refused to humble themselves.

How was Christ to bring these poor souls where Satan would not gain over them a decided victory? How could He show that a mere profession of discipleship did not make them disciples, or insure them a place in His kingdom? How could He show that it is loving service, true humility, which constitutes real greatness? How was He to kindle love in their hearts, and enable them to comprehend what He longed to tell them?

The disciples made no move toward serving one another. Jesus waited for a time to see what they would do. Then He, the divine Teacher, rose from the table. Laying aside the outer garment that would have impeded His movements, He took a towel, and girded Himself. With surprised interest the disciples looked on, and in silence waited to see what was to follow. "After that He poureth water into a basin, and began to wash the disciples' feet, and to wipe them with the towel wherewith He was girded." This action opened the eyes of the disciples. Bitter shame and humiliation filled their hearts. They understood the unspoken rebuke, and saw themselves in altogether a new light.

So Christ expressed His love for His disciples. Their selfish spirit filled Him with sorrow, but He entered into no controversy with them regarding their difficulty. Instead He gave them an example they would never forget. His love for them was not easily disturbed or quenched. He knew that the Father had given all things into His hands, and that He came from God, and went to God. He had a full consciousness of His divinity; but He had laid aside His royal crown and kingly robes, and had taken the form of a servant. One of the last acts of His life on earth was to gird Himself as a servant, and perform a servant's part.

Before the Passover Judas had met a second time with the priests and scribes, and had closed the contract to deliver Jesus into their hands. Yet he afterward mingled with the disciples as though innocent of any wrong, and interested in the work of preparing for the feast. The disciples knew nothing of the purpose of Judas. Jesus alone could read his secret. Yet He did not expose him. Jesus hungered for his soul. He felt for him such a burden as for Jerusalem when He wept over the doomed city. His heart was crying, How can I give thee up? The constraining power of that love was felt by Judas. When the Saviour's hands were bathing those soiled feet, and wiping them with the towel, the heart of Judas thrilled through and through with the impulse then and there to confess his sin. But he would not humble himself. He hardened his heart against repentance; and the old impulses, for the moment put aside, again controlled him. Judas was now offended at Christ's act in washing the feet of His disciples. If Jesus could so humble Himself, he thought, He could not be Israel's king. All hope of worldly honor in a temporal kingdom was destroyed. Judas was satisfied that there was nothing to be gained by following Christ. After seeing Him degrade Himself, as he thought, he was confirmed in his purpose to disown Him, and confess himself deceived. He was possessed by a demon, and he resolved to complete the work he had agreed to do in betraying his Lord.

Judas, in choosing his position at table, had tried to place himself first, and Christ as a servant served him first. John, toward whom Judas had felt so much bitterness, was left till the last. But John did not take this as a rebuke or slight. As the disciples watched Christ's action, they were greatly moved. When Peter's turn came, he exclaimed with astonishment, "Lord, dost Thou wash my feet?" Christ's condescension broke his heart. He was filled with shame to think that one of the disciples was not performing this service. "What I do," Christ said, "thou knowest not now; but thou shalt know hereafter." Peter could not bear to see his Lord, whom he believed to be the Son of God, acting the part of a servant. His whole soul rose up against this humiliation. He did not realize that for this Christ came into the world. With great emphasis he exclaimed, "Thou shalt never wash my feet."

Solemnly Christ said to Peter, "If I wash thee not, thou hast no part with Me." The service which Peter refused was the type of a higher cleansing. Christ had come to wash the heart from the stain of sin. In refusing to allow Christ to wash his feet, Peter was refusing the higher cleansing included in the lower. He was really rejecting his Lord. It is not humiliating to the Master to allow Him to work for our purification. The truest humility is to receive with thankful heart any provision made in our behalf, and with earnestness do service for Christ.

At the words, "If I wash thee not, thou hast no part with Me," Peter surrendered his pride and self-will. He could not endure the thought of separation from Christ; that would have been death to him. "Not my feet only," he said, "but also my hands and my head. Jesus saith to him, He that is washed needeth not save to wash his feet, but is clean every whit."

These words mean more than bodily cleanliness. Christ is still speaking of the higher cleansing as illustrated by the lower. He who came from the bath was clean, but the sandaled feet soon became dusty, and again needed to be washed. So Peter and his brethren had been washed in the great fountain opened for sin and uncleanness. Christ acknowledged them as His. But temptation had led them into evil, and they still needed His cleansing grace. When Jesus girded Himself with a towel to wash the dust from their feet, He desired by that very act to wash the alienation, jealousy, and pride from their hearts. This was of far more consequence than the washing of their dusty feet. With the spirit they then had, not one of them was prepared for communion with Christ. Until brought into a state of humility and love, they were not prepared to partake of the paschal supper, or to share in the memorial service which Christ was about to institute. Their hearts must be cleansed. Pride and self-seeking create dissension and hatred, but all this Jesus washed away in washing their feet. A change of feeling was brought about. Looking upon them, Jesus could say, "Ye are clean." Now there was union of heart, love for one another. They had become humble and teachable. Except Judas, each was ready to concede to another the highest place. Now with subdued and grateful hearts they could receive Christ's words.

Like Peter and his brethren, we too have been washed in the blood of Christ, yet often through contact with evil the heart's purity is soiled. We must come to Christ for His cleansing grace. Peter shrank from bringing his soiled feet in contact with the hands of his Lord and Master; but how often we bring our sinful, polluted hearts in contact with the heart of Christ! How grievous to Him is our evil temper, our vanity and pride! Yet all our infirmity and defilement we must bring to Him. He alone can wash us clean. We are not prepared for communion with Him unless cleansed by His efficacy.

Jesus said to the disciples, "Ye are clean, but not all." He had washed the feet of Judas, but the heart had not been yielded to Him. It was not purified. Judas had not submitted himself to Christ.

After Christ had washed the disciples' feet, and had taken His garments and sat down again, He said to them, "Know ye what I have done to you? Ye call Me Master and Lord: and ye say well; for so I am. If I then, your Lord and Master, have washed your feet; ye also ought to wash one another's feet. For I have given you an example, that ye should do as I have done to you. Verily, verily, I say unto you, The servant is not greater than his lord; neither he that is sent greater than he that sent him."

Christ would have His disciples understand that although He had washed their feet, this did not in the least detract from His dignity. "Ye call Me Master and Lord: and ye say well; for so I am." And being so infinitely superior, He imparted grace and significance to the service. No one was so exalted as Christ, and yet He stooped to the humblest duty. That His people might not be misled by the selfishness which dwells in the natural heart, and which strengthens by self-serving, Christ Himself set the example of humility. He would not leave this great subject in man's charge. Of so much consequence did He regard it, that He Himself, One equal with God, acted as servant to His disciples. While they were contending for the highest place, He to whom every knee shall bow, He whom the angels of glory count it honor to serve, bowed down to wash the feet of those who called Him Lord. He washed the feet of His betrayer.

In His life and lessons, Christ has given a perfect exemplification of the unselfish ministry which has its origin in God. God does not live for Himself. By creating the world, and by upholding all things, He is constantly ministering for others. "He maketh His sun to rise on the evil and on the good, and sendeth rain on the just and on the unjust." Matt. 5:45. This ideal of ministry God has committed to His Son. Jesus was given to stand at the head of humanity, that by His example He might teach what it means to minister. His whole life was under a law of service. He served all, ministered to all. Thus He lived the law of God, and by His example showed how we are to obey it.

Again and again Jesus had tried to establish this principle among His disciples. When James and John made their request for pre-eminence, He had said, "Whosoever will be great among you, let him be your minister." Matt. 20:26. In My kingdom the principle of preference and supremacy has no place. The only greatness is the greatness of humility. The only distinction is found in devotion to the service of others.

Now, having washed the disciples' feet, He said, "I have given you an example, that ye should do as I have done to you." In these words Christ was not merely enjoining the practice of hospitality. More was meant than the washing of the feet of guests to remove the dust of travel. Christ was here instituting a religious service. By the act of our Lord this humiliating ceremony was made a consecrated ordinance. It was to be observed by the disciples, that they might ever keep in mind His lessons of humility and service.

This ordinance is Christ's appointed preparation for the sacramental service. While pride, variance, and strife for supremacy are cherished, the heart cannot enter into fellowship with Christ. We are not prepared to receive the communion of His body and His blood. Therefore it was that Jesus appointed the memorial of His humiliation to be first observed.

As they come to this ordinance, the children of God should bring to remembrance the words of the Lord of life and glory: "Know ye what I have done to you? Ye call Me Master and Lord: and ye say well; for so I am. If I then, your Lord and Master, have washed your feet; ye also ought to wash one another's feet. For I have given you an example, that ye should do as I have done to you. Verily, verily, I say unto you, The servant is not greater than his lord; neither he that is sent greater than he that sent him. If ye know these things, happy are ye if ye do them." There is in man a disposition to esteem himself more highly than his brother, to work for self, to seek the highest place; and often this results in evil surmisings and bitterness of spirit. The ordinance preceding the Lord's Supper is to clear away these misunderstandings, to bring man out of his selfishness, down from his stilts of self-exaltation, to the humility of heart that will lead him to serve his brother.

The holy Watcher from heaven is present at this season to make it one of soul searching, of conviction of sin, and of the blessed assurance of sins forgiven. Christ in the fullness of His grace is there to change the current of the thoughts that have been running in selfish channels. The Holy Spirit quickens the sensibilities of those who follow the example of their Lord. As the Saviour's humiliation for us is remembered, thought links with thought; a chain of memories is called up, memories of God's great goodness and of the favor and tenderness of earthly friends. Blessings forgotten, mercies abused, kindnesses slighted, are called to mind. Roots of bitterness that have crowded out the precious plant of love are made manifest. Defects of character, neglect of duties, ingratitude to God, coldness toward our brethren, are called to remembrance. Sin is seen in the light in which God views it. Our thoughts are not thoughts of self-complacency, but of severe self-censure and humiliation. The mind is energized to break down every barrier that has caused alienation. Evil thinking and evilspeaking are put away. Sins are confessed, they are forgiven. The subduing grace of Christ comes into the soul, and the love of Christ draws hearts together in a blessed unity.

As the lesson of the preparatory service is thus learned, the desire is kindled for a higher spiritual life. To this desire the divine Witness will respond. The soul will be uplifted. We can partake of the Communion with a consciousness of sins forgiven. The sunshine of Christ's righteousness will fill the chambers of the mind and the soul temple. We "behold the Lamb of God, which taketh away the sin of the world." John 1:29.

To those who receive the spirit of this service, it can never become a mere ceremonial. Its constant lesson will be, "By love serve one another." Gal. 5:13. In washing the feet of His disciples, Christ gave evidence that He would do any service, however humble, that would make them heirs with Him of the eternal wealth of heaven's treasure. His disciples, in performing the same rite, pledge themselves in like manner to serve their brethren. Whenever this ordinance is rightly celebrated, the children of God are brought into a holy relationship, to help and bless each other. They covenant that the life shall be given to unselfish ministry. And this, not only for one another. Their field of labor is as wide as their Master's was. The world is full of those who need our ministry. The poor, the helpless, the ignorant, are on every hand. Those who have communed with Christ in the upper chamber will go forth to minister as He did.

Jesus, the served of all, came to be the servant of all. And because He ministered to all, He will again be served and honored by all. And those who would partake of His divine attributes, and share with Him the joy of seeing souls redeemed, must follow His example of unselfish ministry.

All this was comprehended in the words of Jesus, "I have given you an example, that ye should do as I have done to you." This was the intent of the service He established. And He says, "If ye know these things," if you know the purpose of His lessons, "happy are ye if ye do them."

16

"In Remembrance of Me"

This chapter is based on Matthew 26:20-29;
Mark 14:17-25; Luke 22:14-23; John 13:18-30.

"The Lord Jesus the same night in which He was betrayed took bread: and when He had given thanks, He brake it, and said, Take, eat: this is My body, which is broken for you: this do in remembrance of Me. After the same manner also He took the cup, when He had supped, saying, This cup is the new testament in My blood: this do ye, as oft as ye drink it, in remembrance of Me. For as often as ye eat this bread, and drink this cup, ye do show the Lord's death till He come." 1 Cor. 11:23-26.

Christ was standing at the point of transition between two economies and their two great festivals. He, the spotless Lamb of God, was about to present Himself as a sin offering, that He would thus bring to an end the system of types and ceremonies that for four thousand years had pointed to His death. As He ate the Passover with His disciples, He instituted in its place the service that was to be the memorial of His great sacrifice. The national festival of the Jews was to pass away forever. The service which Christ established was to be observed by His followers in all lands and through all ages.

The Passover was ordained as a commemoration of the deliverance of Israel from Egyptian bondage. God had directed that, year by year, as the children should ask the meaning of this ordinance, the history should be repeated. Thus the wonderful deliverance was to be kept fresh in the minds of all. The ordinance of the Lord's Supper was given to commemorate the great deliverance wrought out as the result of the death of Christ. Till He shall come the second time in power and glory, this ordinance is to be celebrated. It is the means by which His great work for us is to be kept fresh in our minds.

At the time of their deliverance from Egypt, the children of Israel ate the Passover supper standing, with their loins girded, and with their staves in their hands, ready for their journey. The manner in which they celebrated this ordinance harmonized with their condition; for they were about to be thrust out of the land of Egypt, and were to begin a painful and difficult journey through the wilderness. But in Christ's time the condition of things had changed. They were not now about to be thrust out of a strange country, but were dwellers in their own land. In harmony with the rest that had been given them, the people then partook of the Passover supper in a reclining position. Couches were placed about the table, and the guests lay upon them, resting upon the left arm, and having the right hand free for use in eating. In this position a guest could lay his head upon the breast of the one who sat next above him. And the feet, being at the outer edge of the couch, could be washed by one passing around the outside of the circle.

Christ is still at the table on which the paschal supper has been spread. The unleavened cakes used at the Passover season are before Him. The Passover wine, untouched by fermentation, is on the table. These emblems Christ employs to represent His own unblemished sacrifice. Nothing corrupted by fermentation, the symbol of sin and death, could represent the "Lamb without blemish and without spot." 1 Peter 1:19.

"And as they were eating, Jesus took bread, and blessed it, and brake it, and gave it to the disciples, and said, Take, eat; this is My body. And He took the cup, and gave thanks, and gave it to them, saying, Drink ye all of it; for this is My blood of the new testament, which is shed for many for the remission of sins. But I say unto you, I will not drink henceforth of this fruit of the vine, until that day when I drink it new with you in My Father's kingdom."

Judas the betrayer was present at the sacramental service. He received from Jesus the emblems of His broken body and His spilled blood. He heard the words, "This do in remembrance of Me." And sitting there in the very presence of the Lamb of God, the betrayer brooded upon his own dark purposes, and cherished his sullen, revengeful thoughts.

At the feet washing, Christ had given convincing proof that He understood the character of Judas. "Ye are not all clean" (John 13:11), He said. These words convinced the false disciple that Christ read his secret purpose. Now Christ spoke out more plainly. As they were seated at the table He said, looking upon His disciples, "I speak not of you all: I know whom I have chosen: but that the scripture may be fulfilled, He that eateth bread with Me hath lifted up his heel against Me."

Even now the disciples did not suspect Judas. But they saw that Christ appeared greatly troubled. A cloud settled over them all, a premonition of some dreadful calamity, the nature of which they did not understand. As they ate in silence, Jesus said, "Verily I say unto you, that one of you shall betray Me." At these words amazement and consternation seized them. They could not comprehend how any one of them could deal treacherously with their divine Teacher. For what cause could they betray Him? and to whom? Whose heart could give birth to such a design? Surely not one of the favored twelve, who had been privileged above all others to hear His teachings, who had shared His wonderful love, and for whom

He had shown such great regard by bringing them into close communion with Himself!

As they realized the import of His words, and remembered how true His sayings were, fear and self-distrust seized them. They began to search their own hearts to see if one thought against their Master were harbored there. With the most painful emotion, one after another inquired, "Lord, is it I?" But Judas sat silent. John in deep distress at last inquired, "Lord, who is it?" And Jesus answered, "He that dippeth his hand with Me in the dish, the same shall betray Me. The Son of man goeth as it is written of Him: but woe unto that man by whom the Son of man is betrayed! it had been good for that man if he had not been born." The disciples had searched one another's faces closely as they asked, "Lord, is it I?" And now the silence of Judas drew all eyes to him. Amid the confusion of questions and expressions of astonishment, Judas had not heard the words of Jesus in answer to John's question. But now, to escape the scrutiny of the disciples, he asked as they had done, "Master, is it I?" Jesus solemnly replied, "Thou hast said."

In surprise and confusion at the exposure of his purpose, Judas rose hastily to leave the room. "Then said Jesus unto him, That thou doest, do quickly. ... He then having received the sop went immediately out: and it was night." Night it was to the traitor as he turned away from Christ into the outer darkness.

Until this step was taken, Judas had not passed beyond the possibility of repentance. But when he left the presence of his Lord and his fellow disciples, the final decision had been made. He had passed the boundary line.

Wonderful had been the long-suffering of Jesus in His dealing with this tempted soul. Nothing that could be done to save Judas had been left undone. After he had twice covenanted to betray his Lord, Jesus still gave him opportunity for repentance. By reading the secret purpose of the traitor's heart, Christ gave to Judas the final, convincing evidence of His divinity. This was to the false disciple the last call to repentance. No appeal that the divine-human heart of Christ could make had been spared. The waves of mercy, beaten back by stubborn pride, returned in a stronger tide of subduing love. But although surprised and alarmed at the discovery of his guilt, Judas became only the more determined. From the sacramental supper he went out to complete the work of betrayal.

In pronouncing the woe upon Judas, Christ also had a purpose of mercy toward His disciples. He thus gave them the crowning evidence of His Messiahship. "I tell you before it come," He said, "that, when it is come to pass, ye may believe that I AM." Had Jesus remained silent, in apparent ignorance of what was to come upon Him, the disciples might have thought that their Master had not divine foresight, and had been sur-prised and betrayed into the hands of the murderous mob. A year before, Jesus had told the disciples that He had chosen twelve, and that one was a devil. Now His words to Judas, showing that his treachery was fully known to his Master, would strengthen the faith of Christ's true followers during His humiliation. And when Judas should have come to his dread-ful end, they would remember the woe that Jesus had pronounced upon the betrayer.

And the Saviour had still another purpose. He had not withheld His ministry from him whom He knew to be a traitor. The disciples did not understand His words when He said at the feet washing, "Ye are not all clean," nor yet when at the table He declared, "He that eateth bread with Me hath lifted up his heel against Me." John 13:11, 18. But afterward, when His meaning was made plain, they had something to consider as to the patience and mercy of God toward the most grievously erring.

Though Jesus knew Judas from the beginning, He washed his feet. And the betrayer was privileged to unite with Christ in partaking of the sacrament. A long-suffering Saviour held out every inducement for the sinner to receive Him, to repent, and to be cleansed from the defilement of sin. This example is for us. When we suppose one to be in error and sin, we are not to divorce ourselves from him. By no careless separation are we to leave him a prey to temptation, or drive him upon Satan's battleground. This is not Christ's method. It was because the disciples were erring and faulty that He washed their feet, and all but one of the twelve were thus brought to repentance.

Christ's example forbids exclusiveness at the Lord's Supper. It is true that open sin excludes the guilty. This the Holy Spirit plainly teaches. 1 Cor. 5:11. But beyond this none are to pass judgment. God has not left it with men to say who shall present themselves on these occasions. For who can read the heart? Who can distinguish the tares from the wheat? "Let a man examine himself, and so let him eat of that bread, and drink of that cup." For "whosoever shall eat this bread, and drink this cup of the Lord, unworthily, shall be guilty of the body and blood of the Lord." "He that eateth and drinketh unworthily, eateth and drinketh damnation to himself, not discerning the Lord's body." 1 Cor. 11:28, 27, 29.

When believers assemble to celebrate the ordinances, there are present messengers unseen by human eyes. There may be a Judas in the company, and if so, messengers from the prince of darkness are there, for they attend all who refuse to be controlled by the Holy Spirit. Heavenly angels also are present. These unseen visitants are present on every such occasion. There may come into the company persons who are not in heart servants of truth and holiness, but who may wish to take part in the service. They should not be forbidden. There are witnesses present who were present when Jesus washed the feet of the disciples and of Judas. More than human eyes beheld the scene.

Christ by the Holy Spirit is there to set the seal to His own ordinance. He is there to convict and soften the heart. Not a look, not a thought of contrition, escapes His notice. For the repentant, brokenhearted one He is waiting. All things are ready for that soul's reception. He who washed the feet of Judas longs to wash every heart from the stain of sin.

None should exclude themselves from the Communion because some who are unworthy may be present. Every disciple is called upon to participate publicly, and thus bear witness that he accepts Christ as a personal Saviour. It is at these, His own appointments, that Christ meets His people, and energizes them by His presence. Hearts and hands that are unworthy may even administer the ordinance, yet Christ is there to minister to His children. All who come with their faith fixed upon Him will be greatly blessed. All who neglect these seasons of divine privilege will suffer loss. Of them it may appropriately be said, "Ye are not all clean."

In partaking with His disciples of the bread and wine, Christ pledged Himself to them as their Redeemer. He committed to them the new covenant, by which all who receive Him become children of God, and joint heirs with Christ. By this covenant every blessing that heaven could bestow for this life and the life to come was theirs. This covenant deed was to be ratified with the blood of Christ. And the administration of the Sacrament was to keep before the disciples the infinite sacrifice made for each of them individually as a part of the great whole of fallen humanity.

But the Communion service was not to be a season of sorrowing. This was not its purpose. As the Lord's disciples gather about His table, they are not to remember and lament their shortcomings. They are not to dwell upon their past religious experience, whether that experience has been elevating or depressing. They are not to recall the differences between them and their brethren. The preparatory service has embraced all this. The self-examination, the confession of sin, the reconciling of differences, has all been done. Now they come to meet with Christ. They are not to stand in the shadow of the cross, but in its saving light. They are to open the soul to the bright beams of the Sun of Righteousness. With hearts cleansed by Christ's most precious blood, in full consciousness of His presence, although unseen, they are to hear His words, "Peace I leave with you, My peace I give unto you: not as the world giveth, give I unto you." John 14:27.

Our Lord says, Under conviction of sin, remember that I died for you. When oppressed and persecuted and afflicted for My sake and the gospel's, remember My love, so great that for you I gave My life. When your duties appear stern and severe, and your burdens too heavy to bear, remember that for your sake I endured the cross, despising the shame. When your heart shrinks from the trying ordeal, remember that your Redeemer liveth to make intercession for you.

The Communion service points to Christ's second coming. It was designed to keep this hope vivid in the minds of the disciples. Whenever they met together to commemorate His death, they recounted how "He took the cup, and gave thanks, and gave it to them, saying, Drink ye all of it; for this is My blood of the new testament, which is shed for many for the remission of sins. But I say unto you, I will not drink henceforth of this fruit of the vine, until that day when I drink it new with you in My Father's kingdom." In their tribulation they found comfort in the hope of their Lord's return. Unspeakably precious to them was the thought, "As often as ye eat this bread, and drink this cup, ye do show the Lord's death till He come." 1 Cor. 11:26.

These are the things we are never to forget. The love of Jesus, with its constraining power, is to be kept fresh in our memory. Christ has instituted this service that it may speak to our senses of the love of God that has been expressed in our behalf. There can be no union between our souls and God except through Christ. The union and love between brother and brother must be cemented and rendered eternal by the love of Jesus. And nothing less than the death of Christ could make His love efficacious for us. It is only because of His death that we can look with joy to His second coming. His sacrifice is the center of our hope. Upon this we must fix our faith.

The ordinances that point to our Lord's humiliation and suffering are regarded too much as a form. They were instituted for a purpose. Our senses need to be quickened to lay hold of the mystery of godliness. It is the privilege of all to comprehend, far more than we do, the expiatory sufferings of Christ. "As Moses lifted up the serpent in the wilderness," even so has the Son of man been lifted up, "that whosoever believeth in Him should not perish, but have eternal life." John 3:14, 15. To the cross of Calvary, bearing a dying Saviour, we must look. Our eternal interests demand that we show faith in Christ.

Our Lord has said, "Except ye eat the flesh of the Son of man, and drink His blood, ye have no life in you. ... For My flesh is meat indeed, and My blood is drink indeed." John 6:53-55. This is true of our physical nature. To the death of Christ we owe even this earthly life. The bread we eat is the purchase of His broken body. The water we drink is bought by His spilled blood. Never one, saint or sinner, eats his daily food, but he is nourished by the body and the blood of Christ. The cross of Calvary is stamped on every loaf. It is reflected in every water spring. All this Christ has taught in appointing the emblems of His great sacrifice. The light shining from that Communion service in the upper chamber makes sacred the provisions for our daily life. The family board becomes as the table of the Lord, and every meal a sacrament.

And how much more are Christ's words true of our spiritual nature. He declares, "Whoso eateth My flesh, and drinketh My blood, hath eternal life." It is by receiving the life for us poured out on Calvary's cross, that we can live the life of holiness. And this life we receive by receiving His word, by doing those things which He has commanded. Thus we become one with Him. "He that eateth My flesh," He says, "and drinketh My blood, dwelleth in Me, and I in him. As the living Father hath sent Me, and I live by the Father: so he that eateth Me, even he shall live by Me." John 6:54, 56, 57. To the holy Communion this scripture in a special sense applies. As faith contemplates our Lord's great sacrifice, the soul assimilates the spiritual life of Christ. That soul will receive spiritual strength from every Communion. The service forms a living connection by which the believer is bound up with Christ, and thus bound up with the Father. In a special sense it forms a connection between dependent human beings and God.

As we receive the bread and wine symbolizing Christ's broken body and spilled blood, we in imagination join in the scene of Communion in the upper chamber. We seem to be passing through the garden consecrated by the agony of Him who bore the sins of the world. We witness the struggle by which our reconciliation with God was obtained. Christ is set forth crucified among us.

Looking upon the crucified Redeemer, we more fully comprehend the magnitude and meaning of the sacrifice made by the Majesty of heaven. The plan of salvation is glorified before us, and the thought of Calvary awakens living and sacred emotions in our hearts. Praise to God and the Lamb will be in our hearts and on our lips; for pride and self-worship cannot flourish in the soul that keeps fresh in memory the scenes of Calvary.

He who beholds the Saviour's matchless love will be elevated in thought, purified in heart, transformed in character. He will go forth to be a light to the world, to reflect in some degree this mysterious love. The more we contemplate the cross of Christ, the more fully shall we adopt the language of the apostle when he said, "God forbid that I should glory, save in the cross of our Lord Jesus Christ, by whom the world is crucified unto me, and I unto the world." Gal. 6:14

17

"Let Not Your Heart Be Troubled"

This chapter is based on John 13:31-38; 14-17.

Looking upon His disciples with divine love and with the tenderest sympathy, Christ said, "Now is the Son of man glorified, and God is glorified in Him." Judas had left the upper chamber, and Christ was alone with the eleven. He was about to speak of His approaching separation from them; but before doing this He pointed to the great object of His mission. It was this that He kept ever before Him. It was His joy that all His humiliation and suffering would glorify the Father's name. To this He first directs the thoughts of His disciples.

Then addressing them by the endearing term, "Little children," He said, "Yet a little while I am with you. Ye shall seek Me: and as I said unto the Jews, Whither I go, ye cannot come; so now I say to you."

The disciples could not rejoice when they heard this. Fear fell upon them. They pressed close about the Saviour. Their Master and Lord, their beloved Teacher and Friend, He was dearer to them than life. To Him they had looked for help in all their difficulties, for comfort in their sorrows and disappointments. Now He was to leave them, a lonely, dependent company. Dark were the forebodings that filled their hearts.

But the Saviour's words to them were full of hope. He knew that they were to be assailed by the enemy, and that Satan's craft is most successful against those who are depressed by difficulties. Therefore He pointed them away from "the things which are seen," to "the things which are not seen." 2 Cor. 4:18. From earthly exile He turned their thoughts to the heavenly home.

"Let not your heart be troubled," He said; "ye believe in God, believe also in Me. In My Father's house are many mansions: if it were not so, I would have told you. I go to prepare a place for you. And if I go and prepare a place for you, I will come again, and receive you unto Myself; that where I am, there ye may be also. And whither I go ye know, and the way ye know." For your sake I came into the world. I am working in your behalf. When I go away, I shall still work earnestly for you. I came into the world to reveal Myself to you, that you might believe. I go to the Father to co-operate with Him in your behalf. The object of Christ's departure was the opposite of what the disciples feared. It did not mean a final separation. He was going to prepare a place for them, that He might come again, and receive them unto Himself. While He was building mansions for them, they were to build characters after the divine similitude.

Still the disciples were perplexed. Thomas, always troubled by doubts, said, "Lord, we know not whither Thou goest; and how can we know the way? Jesus saith unto him, I am the way, the truth, and the life; no man cometh unto the Father, but by Me. If ye had known Me, ye should have known My Father also: and from henceforth ye know Him, and have seen Him."

There are not many ways to heaven. Each one may not choose his own way. Christ says, "I am the way: ... no man cometh unto the Father, but by Me." Since the first gospel sermon was preached, when in Eden it was declared that the seed of the woman should bruise the serpent's head, Christ had been uplifted as the way, the truth, and the life. He was the way when Adam lived, when Abel presented to God the blood of the slain lamb, representing the blood of the Redeemer. Christ was the way by which patriarchs and prophets were saved. He is the way by which alone we can have access to God.

"If ye had known Me," Christ said, "ye should have known My Father also: and from henceforth ye know Him, and have seen Him." But not yet did the disciples understand. "Lord, show us the Father," exclaimed Philip, "and it sufficeth us."

Amazed at his dullness of comprehension, Christ asked with pained surprise, "Have I been so long time with you, and yet hast thou not known Me, Philip?" Is it possible that you do not see the Father in the works He does through Me? Do you not believe that I came to testify of the Father? "How sayest thou then, Show us the Father?" "He that hath seen Me hath seen the Father." Christ had not ceased to be God when He became man. Though He had humbled Himself to humanity, the Godhead was still His own. Christ alone could represent the Father to humanity, and this representation the disciples had been privileged to behold for over three years.

"Believe Me that I am in the Father, and the Father in Me: or else believe Me for the very works' sake." Their faith might safely rest on the evidence given in Christ's works, works that no man, of himself, ever had done, or ever could do. Christ's work testified to His divinity. Through Him the Father had been revealed.

If the disciples believed this vital connection between the Father and the Son, their faith would not forsake them when they saw Christ's suffering and death to save a perishing world. Christ was seeking to lead them from their low condition of faith to the experience they might receive if they truly realized what He was,—God in human flesh. He desired them to see that their faith must lead up to God, and be anchored there. How earnestly and perseveringly our compassionate Saviour sought to prepare His disciples for the storm of temptation that was soon to beat upon them. He would have them hid with Him in God.

As Christ was speaking these words, the glory of God was shining from His countenance, and all present felt a sacred awe as they listened with rapt attention to His words. Their hearts were more decidedly drawn to Him; and as they were drawn to Christ in greater love, they were drawn to one another. They felt that heaven was very near, and that the words to which they listened were a message to them from their heavenly Father.

"Verily, verily, I say unto you," Christ continued, "He that believeth on Me, the works that I do shall he do also." The Saviour was deeply anxious for His disciples to understand for what purpose His divinity was united to humanity. He came to the world to display the glory of God, that man might be uplifted by its restoring power. God was manifested in Him that He might be manifested in them. Jesus revealed no qualities, and exercised no powers, that men may not have through faith in Him. His perfect humanity is that which all His followers may possess, if they will be in subjection to God as He was.

"And greater works than these shall he do; because I go unto My Father." By this Christ did not mean that the disciples' work would be of a more exalted character than His, but that it would have greater extent. He did not refer merely to miracle working, but to all that would take place under the working of the Holy Spirit.

After the Lord's ascension, the disciples realized the fulfillment of His promise. The scenes of the crucifixion, resurrection, and ascension of Christ were a living reality to them. They saw that the prophecies had been literally fulfilled. They searched the Scriptures, and accepted their teaching with a faith and assurance unknown before. They knew that the divine Teacher was all that He had claimed to be. As they told their experience, and exalted the love of God, men's hearts were melted and subdued, and multitudes believed on Jesus.

The Saviour's promise to His disciples is a promise to His church to the end of time. God did not design that His wonderful plan to redeem men should achieve only insignificant results. All who will go to work, trusting not in what they themselves can do, but in what God can do for and through them, will certainly realize the fulfillment of His promise. "Greater works than these shall ye do," He declares; "because I go unto My Father."

As yet the disciples were unacquainted with the Saviour's unlimited resources and power. He said to them, "Hitherto have ye asked nothing in My name." John 16:24. He explained that the secret of their success would be in asking for strength and grace in His name. He would be present before the Father to make request for them. The prayer of the humble suppliant He presents as His own desire in that soul's behalf. Every sincere prayer is heard in heaven. It may not be fluently expressed; but if the heart is in it, it will ascend to the sanctuary where Jesus ministers, and He will present it to the Father without one awkward, stammering word, beautiful and fragrant with the incense of His own perfection.

The path of sincerity and integrity is not a path free from obstruction, but in every difficulty we are to see a call to prayer. There is no one living who has any power that he has not received from God, and the source whence it comes is open to the weakest human being. "Whatsoever ye shall ask in My name," said Jesus, "that will I do, that the Father may be glorified in the Son. If ye shall ask anything in My name, I will do it."

"In My name," Christ bade His disciples pray. In Christ's name His followers are to stand before God. Through the value of the sacrifice made for them, they are of value in the Lord's sight. Because of the imputed righteousness of Christ they are accounted precious. For Christ's sake the Lord pardons those that fear Him. He does not see in them the vileness of the sinner. He recognizes in them the likeness of His Son, in whom they believe.

The Lord is disappointed when His people place a low estimate upon themselves. He desires His chosen heritage to value themselves according to the price He has placed upon them. God wanted them, else He would not have sent His Son on such an expensive errand to redeem them. He has a use for them, and He is well pleased when they make the very highest demands upon Him, that they may glorify His name. They may expect large things if they have faith in His promises.

But to pray in Christ's name means much. It means that we are to accept His character, manifest His spirit, and work His works. The Saviour's promise is given on condition. "If ye love Me," He says, "keep My commandments." He saves men, not in sin, but from sin; and those who love Him will show their love by obedience.

All true obedience comes from the heart. It was heart work with Christ. And if we consent, He will so identify Himself with our thoughts and aims, so blend our hearts and minds into conformity to His will, that when obeying Him we shall be but carrying out our own impulses. The will, refined and sanctified, will find its highest delight in doing His service. When we know God as it is our privilege to know Him, our life will be a life of continual obedience. Through an appreciation of the character of Christ, through communion with God, sin will become hateful to us.

As Christ lived the law in humanity, so we may do if we will take hold of the Strong for strength. But we are not to place the responsibility of our duty upon others, and wait for them to tell us what to do. We cannot depend for counsel upon humanity. The Lord will teach us our duty just as willingly as He will teach somebody else. If we come to Him in faith, He will speak His mysteries to us personally. Our hearts will often burn within us as One draws nigh to commune with us as He did with Enoch. Those who decide to do nothing in any line that will displease God, will know, after presenting their case before Him, just what course to pursue. And they will receive not only wisdom, but strength. Power for obedience, for service, will be imparted to them, as Christ has promised. Whatever was given to Christ—the "all things" to supply the need of fallen men—was given to Him as the head and representative of humanity. And "whatsoever we ask, we receive of Him, because we keep His commandments, and do those things that are pleasing in His sight." 1 John 3:22.

Before offering Himself as the sacrificial victim, Christ sought for the most essential and complete gift to bestow upon His followers, a gift that would bring within their reach the boundless resources of grace. "I will pray the Father," He said, "and He shall give you another Comforter, that He may abide with you forever; even the Spirit of truth; whom the world cannot receive, because it seeth Him not, neither knoweth Him: but ye know Him; for He dwelleth with you, and shall be in you. I will not leave you orphans: I will come to you." John 14:16-18, margin.

Before this the Spirit had been in the world; from the very beginning of the work of redemption He had been moving upon men's hearts. But while Christ was on earth, the disciples had desired no other helper. Not until they were deprived of His presence would they feel their need of the Spirit, and then He would come.

The Holy Spirit is Christ's representative, but divested of the personality of humanity, and independent thereof. Cumbered with humanity, Christ could not be in every place personally. Therefore it was for their interest that He should go to the Father, and send the Spirit to be His successor on earth. No one could then have any advantage because of his location or his personal contact with Christ. By the Spirit the Saviour would be accessible to all. In this sense He would be nearer to them than if He had not ascended on high.

"He that loveth Me shall be loved of My Father, and I will love him, and will manifest Myself to him." Jesus read the future of His disciples. He saw one brought to the scaffold, one to the cross, one to exile among the lonely rocks of the sea, others to persecution and death. He encouraged them with the promise that in every trial He would be with them. That promise has lost none of its force. The Lord knows all about His faithful servants who for His sake are lying in prison or who are banished to lonely islands. He comforts them with His own presence. When for the truth's sake the believer stands at the bar of unrighteous tribunals, Christ stands by his side. All the reproaches that fall upon him, fall upon Christ. Christ is condemned over again in the person of His disciple. When one is incarcerated in prison walls, Christ ravishes the heart with His love. When one suffers death for His sake, Christ says, "I am He that liveth, and was dead; and, behold, I am alive forevermore, ... and have the keys of hell and of death." Rev. 1:18. The life that is sacrificed for Me is preserved unto eternal glory.

At all times and in all places, in all sorrows and in all afflictions, when the outlook seems dark and the future perplexing, and we feel helpless and alone, the Comforter will be sent in answer to the prayer of faith. Circumstances may separate us from every earthly friend; but no circumstance, no distance, can separate us from the heavenly Comforter. Wherever we are, wherever we may go, He is always at our right hand to support, sustain, uphold, and cheer.

The disciples still failed to understand Christ's words in their spiritual sense, and again He explained His meaning. By the Spirit, He said, He would manifest Himself to them. "The Comforter, which is the Holy Ghost, whom the Father will send in My name, He shall teach you all things." No more will you say, I cannot comprehend. No longer will you see through a glass, darkly. You shall "be able to comprehend with all saints what is the breadth, and length, and depth, and height; and to know the love of Christ, which passeth knowledge." Eph. 3:18, 19.

The disciples were to bear witness to the life and work of Christ. Through their word He was to speak to all the people on the face of the earth. But in the humiliation and death of Christ they were to suffer great trial and disappointment. That after this experience their word might be accurate, Jesus promised that the Comforter should "bring all things to your remembrance, whatsoever I have said unto you."

"I have yet many things to say unto you," He continued, "but ye cannot bear them now. Howbeit when He, the Spirit of truth, is come, He will guide you into all truth: for He shall not speak of Himself; but whatsoever He shall hear, that shall He speak: and He will show you things to come. He shall glorify Me: for He shall receive of Mine, and shall show it unto you." Jesus had opened before His disciples a vast tract of truth. But it was most difficult for them to keep His lessons distinct from the traditions and maxims of the scribes and Pharisees. They had been educated to accept the teaching of the rabbis as the voice of God, and it still held a power over their minds, and molded their sentiments. Earthly ideas, temporal things, still had a large place in their thoughts. They did not understand the spiritual nature of Christ's kingdom, though He had so often explained it to them. Their minds had become confused. They did not comprehend the value of the scriptures Christ presented. Many of His lessons seemed almost lost upon them. Jesus saw that they did not lay hold of the real meaning of His words. He compassionately promised that the Holy Spirit should recall these sayings to their minds. And He had left unsaid many things that could not be comprehended by the disciples. These also would be opened to them by the Spirit. The Spirit was to quicken their understanding, that they might have an appreciation of heavenly things. "When He, the Spirit of truth, is come," said Jesus, "He will guide you into all truth."

The Comforter is called "the Spirit of truth." His work is to define and maintain the truth. He first dwells in the heart as the Spirit of truth, and thus He becomes the Comforter. There is comfort and peace in the truth, but no real peace or comfort can be found in falsehood. It is through false theories and traditions that Satan gains his power over the mind. By directing men to false standards, he misshapes the character. Through the Scriptures the Holy Spirit speaks to the mind, and impresses truth upon the heart. Thus He exposes error, and expels it from the soul. It is by the Spirit of truth, working through the word of God, that Christ subdues His chosen people to Himself.

In describing to His disciples the office work of the Holy Spirit, Jesus sought to inspire them with the joy and hope that inspired His own heart. He rejoiced because of the abundant help He had provided for His church. The Holy Spirit was the highest of all gifts that He could solicit from His Father for the exaltation of His people. The Spirit was to be given as a regenerating agent, and without this the sacrifice of Christ would have been of no avail. The power of evil had been strengthening for centuries, and the submission of men to this satanic captivity was amazing. Sin could be resisted and overcome only through the mighty agency of the Third Person of the Godhead, who would come with no modified energy, but in the fullness of divine power. It is the Spirit that makes effectual what has been wrought out by the world's Redeemer. It is by the Spirit that the heart is made pure. Through the Spirit the believer becomes a partaker of the divine nature. Christ has given His Spirit as a divine power to overcome all hereditary and cultivated tendencies to evil, and to impress His own character upon His church.

Of the Spirit Jesus said, "He shall glorify Me." The Saviour came to glorify the Father by the demonstration of His love; so the Spirit was to glorify Christ by revealing His grace to the world. The very image of God is to be reproduced in humanity. The honor of God, the honor of Christ, is involved in the perfection of the character of His people.

"When He [the Spirit of truth] is come, He will reprove the world of sin, and of righteousness, and of judgment." The preaching of the word will be of no avail without the continual presence and aid of the Holy Spirit. This is the only effectual teacher of divine truth. Only when the truth is accompanied to the heart by the Spirit will it quicken the conscience or transform the life. One might be able to present the letter of the word of God, he might be familiar with all its commands and promises; but unless the Holy Spirit sets home the truth, no souls will fall on the Rock and be broken. No amount of education, no advantages, however great, can make one a channel of light without the co-operation of the Spirit of God. The sowing of the gospel seed will not be a success unless the seed is quickened into life by the dew of heaven. Before one book of the New Testament was written, before one gospel sermon had been preached after Christ's ascension, the Holy Spirit came upon the praying apostles. Then the testimony of their enemies was, "Ye have filled Jerusalem with your doctrine." Acts 5:28.

Christ has promised the gift of the Holy Spirit to His church, and the promise belongs to us as much as to the first disciples. But like every other promise, it is given on conditions. There are many who believe and profess to claim the Lord's promise; they talk *about* Christ and *about* the Holy Spirit, yet receive no benefit. They do not surrender the soul to be guided and controlled by the divine agencies. We cannot use the Holy Spirit. The Spirit is to use us. Through the Spirit God works in His people "to will and to do of His good pleasure." Phil. 2:13. But many will not submit to this. They want to manage themselves. This is why they do not receive the heavenly gift. Only to those who wait humbly upon God, who watch for His guidance and grace, is the Spirit given. The power of God awaits their demand and reception. This promised blessing, claimed by faith, brings all other blessings in its train. It is given according to the riches of the grace of Christ, and He is ready to supply every soul according to the capacity to receive.

In His discourse to the disciples, Jesus made no mournful allusion to His own sufferings and death. His last legacy to them was a legacy of peace. He said, "Peace I leave with you, My peace I give unto you: not as the world giveth, give I unto you. Let not your heart be troubled, neither let it be afraid."

Before leaving the upper chamber, the Saviour led His disciples in a song of praise. His voice was heard, not in the strains of some mournful lament, but in the joyful notes of the Passover hallel:

"O praise the Lord, all ye nations:
Praise Him, all ye people.
For His merciful kindness is great toward us:
And the truth of the Lord endureth forever.
Praise ye the Lord." Psalm 117.

After the hymn, they went out. Through the crowded streets they made their way, passing out of the city gate toward the Mount of Olives. Slowly they proceeded, each busy with his own thoughts. As they began to descend toward the mount, Jesus said, in a tone of deepest sadness, "All ye shall be offended because of Me this night: for it is written, I will smite the shepherd, and the sheep of the flock shall be scattered abroad." Matt. 26:31. The disciples listened in sorrow and amazement. They remembered how in the synagogue at Capernaum, when Christ spoke of Himself as the bread of life, many had been offended, and had turned away from Him. But the twelve had not shown themselves unfaithful. Peter, speaking for his brethren, had then declared his loyalty to Christ. Then the Saviour had said, "Have not I chosen you twelve, and one of you is a devil?" John 6:70. In the upper chamber Jesus said that one of the twelve would betray Him, and that Peter would deny Him. But now His words include them all.

Now Peter's voice is heard vehemently protesting, "Although all shall be offended, yet will not I." In the upper chamber he had declared, "I will lay down my life for Thy sake." Jesus had warned him that he would that very night deny his Saviour. Now Christ repeats the warning: "Verily I say unto thee, That this day, even in this night, before the cock crow twice, thou shalt deny Me thrice." But Peter only "spake the more vehemently, If I should die with Thee, I will not deny Thee in anywise. Likewise also said they all." Mark 14:29-31. In their self-confidence they denied the repeated statement of Him who knew. They were unprepared for the test; when temptation should overtake them, they would understand their own weakness.

When Peter said he would follow his Lord to prison and to death, he meant it, every word of it; but he did not know himself. Hidden in his heart were elements of evil that circumstances would fan into life. Unless he was made conscious of his danger, these would prove his eternal ruin. The Saviour saw in him a self-love and assurance that would overbear even his love for Christ. Much of infirmity, of unmortified sin, carelessness of spirit, unsanctified temper, heedlessness in entering into temptation, had been revealed in his experience. Christ's solemn warning was a call to heart searching. Peter needed to distrust himself, and to have a deeper faith in Christ. Had he in humility received the warning, he would have appealed to the Shepherd of the flock to keep His sheep. When on the Sea of Galilee he was about to sink, he cried, "Lord, save me." Matt. 14:30. Then the hand of Christ was outstretched to grasp his hand. So now if he had cried to Jesus, Save me from myself, he would have been kept. But Peter felt that he was distrusted, and he thought it cruel. He was already offended, and he became more persistent in his self-confidence.

Jesus looks with compassion on His disciples. He cannot save them from the trial, but He does not leave them comfortless. He assures them that He is to break the fetters of the tomb, and that His love for them will not fail. "After I am risen again," He says, "I will go before you into Galilee." Matt. 26:32. Before the denial, they have the assurance of forgiveness. After His death and resurrection, they knew that they were forgiven, and were dear to the heart of Christ.

Jesus and the disciples were on the way to Gethsemane, at the foot of Mount Olivet, a retired spot which He had often visited for meditation and prayer. The Saviour had been explaining to His disciples His mission to the world, and the spiritual relation to Him which they were to sustain. Now He illustrates the lesson. The moon is shining bright, and reveals to Him a flourishing grapevine. Drawing the attention of the disciples to it, He employs it as a symbol.

"I am the true Vine," He says. Instead of choosing the graceful palm, the lofty cedar, or the strong oak, Jesus takes the vine with its clinging tendrils to represent Himself. The palm tree, the cedar, and the oak stand alone. They require no support. But the vine entwines about the trellis, and thus climbs heavenward. So Christ in His humanity was dependent upon divine power. "I can of Mine own self do nothing," He declared. John 5:30.

"I am the true Vine." The Jews had always regarded the vine as the most noble of plants, and a type of all that was powerful, excellent, and fruitful. Israel had been represented as a vine which God had planted in the Promised Land. The Jews based their hope of salvation on the fact of their connection with Israel. But Jesus says, I am the real Vine. Think not that through a connection with Israel you may become partakers of the life of God, and inheritors of His promise. Through Me alone is spiritual life received.

"I am the true Vine, and My Father is the husbandman." On the hills of Palestine our heavenly Father had planted this goodly Vine, and He Himself was the husbandman. Many were attracted by the beauty of this Vine, and declared its heavenly origin. But to the leaders in Israel it appeared as a root out of a dry ground. They took the plant, and bruised it, and trampled it under their unholy feet. Their thought was to destroy it forever. But the heavenly Husbandman never lost sight of His plant. After men thought they had killed it, He took it, and replanted it on the other side of the wall. The vine stock was to be no longer visible. It was hidden from the rude assaults of men. But the branches of the Vine hung over the wall. They were to represent the Vine. Through them grafts might still be united to the Vine. From them fruit has been obtained. There has been a harvest which the passers-by have plucked.

"I am the Vine, ye are the branches," Christ said to His disciples. Though He was about to be removed from them, their spiritual union with Him was to be unchanged. The connection of the branch with the vine, He said, represents the relation you are to sustain to Me. The scion is engrafted into the living vine, and fiber by fiber, vein by vein, it grows into the vine stock. The life of the vine becomes the life of the branch. So the soul dead in trespasses and sins receives life through connection with Christ. By faith in Him as a personal Saviour the union is formed. The sinner unites his weakness to Christ's strength, his emptiness to Christ's fullness, his frailty to Christ's enduring might. Then he has the mind of Christ. The humanity of Christ has touched our humanity, and our humanity has touched divinity. Thus through the agency of the Holy Spirit man becomes a partaker of the divine nature. He is accepted in the Beloved.

This union with Christ, once formed, must be maintained. Christ said, "Abide in Me, and I in you. As the branch cannot bear fruit of itself, except it abide in the vine; no more can ye, except ye abide in Me." This is no casual touch, no off-and-on connection. The branch becomes a part of the living vine. The communication of life, strength, and fruitfulness from the root to the branches is unobstructed and constant. Separated from the vine, the branch cannot live. No more, said Jesus, can you live apart from Me. The life you have received from Me can be preserved only by continual communion. Without Me you cannot overcome one sin, or resist one temptation.

"Abide in Me, and I in you." Abiding in Christ means a constant receiving of His Spirit, a life of unreserved surrender to His service. The channel of communication must be open continually between man and his God. As the vine branch constantly draws the sap from the living vine, so are we to cling to Jesus, and receive from Him by faith the strength and perfection of His own character.

The root sends its nourishment through the branch to the outermost twig. So Christ communicates the current of spiritual strength to every believer. So long as the soul is united to Christ, there is no danger that it will wither or decay.

The life of the vine will be manifest in fragrant fruit on the branches. "He that abideth in Me," said Jesus, "and I in him, the same bringeth forth much fruit: for without Me ye can do nothing." When we live by faith on the Son of God, the fruits of the Spirit will be seen in our lives; not one will be missing.

"My Father is the husbandman. Every branch in Me that beareth not fruit He taketh away." While the graft is outwardly united with the vine, there may be no vital connection. Then there will be no growth or fruitfulness. So there may be an apparent connection with Christ without a real union with Him by faith. A profession of religion places men in the church, but the character and conduct show whether they are in connection with Christ. If they bear no fruit, they are false branches. Their separation from Christ involves a ruin as complete as that represented by the dead branch. "If a man abide not in Me," said Christ, "he is cast forth as a branch, and is withered; and men gather them, and cast them into the fire, and they are burned."

"And every branch that beareth fruit, He purgeth [pruneth] it, that it may bring forth more fruit." From the chosen twelve who had followed Jesus, one as a withered branch was about to be taken away; the rest were to pass under the pruning knife of bitter trial. Jesus with solemn tenderness explained the purpose of the husbandman. The pruning will cause pain, but it is the Father who applies the knife. He works with no wanton hand or indifferent heart. There are branches trailing upon the ground; these must be cut loose from the earthly supports to which their tendrils are fastening. They are to reach heavenward, and find their support in God. The excessive foliage that draws away the life current from the fruit must be pruned off. The overgrowth must be cut out, to give room for the healing beams of the Sun of Righteousness. The husbandman prunes away the harmful growth, that the fruit may be richer and more abundant.

"Herein is My Father glorified," said Jesus, "that ye bear much fruit." God desires to manifest through you the holiness, the benevolence, the compassion, of His own character. Yet the Saviour does not bid the disciples labor to bear fruit. He tells them to abide in Him. "If ye abide in Me," He says, "and My words abide in you, ye shall ask what ye will, and it shall be done unto you." It is through the word that Christ abides in His followers. This is the same vital union that is represented by eating His flesh and drinking His blood. The words of Christ are spirit and life. Receiving them, you receive the life of the Vine. You live "by every word that proceedeth out of the mouth of God." Matt. 4:4. The life of Christ in you produces the same fruits as in Him. Living in Christ, adhering to Christ, supported by Christ, drawing nourishment from Christ, you bear fruit after the similitude of Christ.

In this last meeting with His disciples, the great desire which Christ expressed for them was that they might love one another as He had loved them. Again and again He spoke of this. "These things I command you," He said repeatedly, "that ye love one another." His very first injunction when alone with them in the upper chamber was, "A new commandment I give unto you, That ye love one another; as I have loved you, that ye also love one another." To the disciples this commandment was new; for they had not loved one another as Christ had loved them. He saw that new ideas and impulses must control them; that new principles must be practiced by them; through His life and death they were to receive a new conception of love. The command to love one another had a new meaning in the light of His self-sacrifice. The whole work of grace is one continual service of love, of self-denying, self-sacrificing effort. During every hour of Christ's sojourn upon the earth, the love of God was flowing from Him in irrepressible streams. All who are imbued with His Spirit will love as He loved. The very principle that actuated Christ will actuate them in all their dealing one with another.

This love is the evidence of their discipleship. "By this shall all men know that ye are My disciples," said Jesus, "if ye have love one to another." When men are bound together, not by force or self-interest, but by love, they show the working of an influence that is above every human influence. Where this oneness exists, it is evidence that the image of God is being restored in humanity, that a new principle of life has been implanted. It shows that there is power in the divine nature to withstand the supernatural agencies of evil, and that the grace of God subdues the selfishness inherent in the natural heart.

This love, manifested in the church, will surely stir the wrath of Satan. Christ did not mark out for His disciples an easy path. "If the world hate you," He said, "ye know that it hated Me before it hated you. If ye were of the world, the world would love his own: but because ye are not of the world, but I have chosen you out of the world, therefore the world hateth you. Remember the word that I said unto you, The servant is not greater than his lord. If they have persecuted Me, they will also persecute you; if they have kept My saying, they will keep yours also. But all these things will they do unto you for My name's sake, because they know not Him that sent Me." The gospel is to be carried forward by aggressive warfare, in the midst of opposition, peril, loss, and suffering. But those who do this work are only following in their Master's steps.

As the world's Redeemer, Christ was constantly confronted with apparent failure. He, the messenger of mercy to our world, seemed to do little of the work He longed to do in uplifting and saving. Satanic influences were constantly working to oppose His way. But He would not be discouraged. Through the prophecy of Isaiah He declares, "I have labored in vain, I have spent My strength for nought, and in vain: yet surely My judgment is with the Lord, and My work with My God. ... Though Israel be not gathered, yet shall I be glorious in the eyes of the Lord, and My God shall be My strength." It is to Christ that the promise is given, "Thus saith the Lord, the Redeemer of Israel, and His Holy One, to Him whom man despiseth, to Him whom the nation abhorreth; ... thus saith the Lord: ... I will preserve Thee, and give Thee for a covenant of the people, to establish the earth, to cause to inherit the desolate heritages; that Thou mayest say to the prisoners, Go forth; to them that are in darkness, Show yourselves. ... They shall not hunger nor thirst; neither shall the heat nor sun smite them: for He that hath mercy on them shall lead them, even by the springs of water shall He guide them." Isa. 49:4, 5, 7-10.

Upon this word Jesus rested, and He gave Satan no advantage. When the last steps of Christ's humiliation were to be taken, when the deepest sorrow was closing about His soul, He said to His disciples, "The prince of this world cometh, and hath nothing in Me." "The prince of this world is judged." Now shall he be cast out. John 14:30; 16:11; 12:31. With prophetic eye Christ traced the scenes to take place in His last great conflict. He knew that when He should exclaim, "It is finished," all heaven would triumph. His ear caught the distant music and the shouts of victory in the heavenly courts. He knew that the knell of Satan's empire would then be sounded, and the name of Christ would be heralded from world to world throughout the universe.

Christ rejoiced that He could do more for His followers than they could ask or think. He spoke with assurance, knowing that an almighty decree had been given before the world was made. He knew that truth, armed with the omnipotence of the Holy Spirit, would conquer in the contest with evil; and that the bloodstained banner would wave triumphantly over His followers. He knew that the life of His trusting disciples would be like His, a series of uninterrupted victories, not seen to be such here, but recognized as such in the great hereafter.

"These things I have spoken unto you," He said, "that in Me ye might have peace. In the world ye shall have tribulation: but be of good cheer; I have overcome the world." Christ did not fail, neither was He discouraged, and His followers are to manifest a faith of the same enduring nature. They are to live as He lived, and work as He worked, because they depend on Him as the great Master Worker. Courage, energy, and perseverance they must possess. Though apparent impossibilities obstruct their way, by His grace they are to go forward. Instead of deploring difficulties, they are called upon to surmount them. They are to despair of nothing, and to hope for everything. With the golden chain of His matchless love Christ has bound them to the throne of God. It is His purpose that the highest influence in the universe, emanating from the source of all power, shall be theirs. They are to have power to resist evil, power that neither earth, nor death, nor hell can master, power that will enable them to overcome as Christ overcame.

Christ designs that heaven's order, heaven's plan of government, heaven's divine harmony, shall be represented in His church on earth. Thus in His people He is glorified. Through them the Sun of Righteousness will shine in undimmed luster to the world. Christ has given to His church ample facilities, that He may receive a large revenue of glory from His redeemed, purchased possession. He has bestowed upon His people capabilities and blessings that they may represent His own sufficiency. The church, endowed with the righteousness of Christ, is His depositary, in which the riches of His mercy, His grace, and His love, are to appear in full and final display. Christ looks upon His people in their purity and perfection, as the reward of His humiliation, and the supplement of His glory,—Christ, the great Center, from whom radiates all glory.

With strong, hopeful words the Saviour ended His instruction. Then He poured out the burden of His soul in prayer for His disciples. Lifting His eyes to heaven, He said, "Father, the hour is come; glorify Thy Son, that Thy Son also may glorify Thee: as Thou hast given Him power over all flesh, that He should give eternal life to as many as Thou hast given Him. And this is life eternal, that they might know Thee the only true God, and Jesus Christ, whom Thou hast sent."

Christ had finished the work that was given Him to do. He had glorified God on the earth. He had manifested the Father's name. He had gathered out those who were to continue His work among men. And He said, "I am glorified in them. And now I am no more in the world, but these are in the world, and I come to Thee. Holy Father, keep through Thine own name those whom Thou hast given Me, that they may be one, as We are." "Neither pray I for these alone, but for them also which shall believe on Me through their word; that they all may be one; … I in them, and Thou in Me, that they may be made perfect in one; and that the world may know that Thou hast sent Me, and hast loved them, as Thou hast loved Me."

Thus in the language of one who has divine authority, Christ gives His elect church into the Father's arms. As a consecrated high priest He intercedes for His people. As a faithful shepherd He gathers His flock under the shadow of the Almighty, in the strong and sure refuge. For Him there waits the last battle with Satan, and He goes forth to meet it.

Complete Your Set!

| **Born to Die** | **Expect a Miracle** | **The Master of Love** | **Shadow of the Cross** | **The Passion of Love** |
| RP1019 | RP1030 | RP1083 | RP1160 | RP1017 |

It began in a lowly stable in Bethlehem and culminated violently on a hill called Calvary—a brief moment in time that forever changed the world. But nothing you'll see or hear can compare to the gospel truth. Only Bible itself will ever fill you with hope or inspire you more than this collection of books.

Indeed, no picture, or film or sound will match the breathtaking detail and power of this beautiful set taken from the best-selling masterpiece *The Desire of Ages*. This vibrant and biblically faithful commentary documents the life of Jesus Christ from the promise of His birth through the time of His ascension into the clouds bound for His Father's throne.

This gripping and unique narrative from one of Christianity's most-published writers takes you through the life of Christ and goes beyond the physical suffering and explores the deeper spiritual revelation of love's most poignant act. You'll understand more about the intricacies of Jesus' life, ministry, and suffering as you never have before. Complete your set today and complete your journey now!

Full Set in One Volume

This special edition book contains all five books of the series under one cover. You will also find several chapters that were not included in the 5-book set. This must-read masterpiece has given knowledge and assurance to millions. Now it's your turn to have the answers you need to face the future.

Call Now 1-800-423-1319 or visit www.RemnantPublications.com

Scriptural Index